Get Your Coat, You're Nicked!

The Life of a Drug Detective and Special Agent

Get Your Coat, You're Nicked!

The Life of a Drug Detective and Special Agent

CLIVE 'YAKI' BRIND

Text Stefanie Fox, on behalf of StoryTerrace
Copyright © Clive 'Yaki' Brind

First print December 2023

CONTENTS

FOREWORD — 7

CHAPTER 1: FROM SCOUTS TO THE FORCE — 9

CHAPTER 2: NEWLY HATCHED — 19

CHAPTER 3: A JOURNEY IN BLUE — 31

CHAPTER 4: RIGHTING WRONGS — 39

CHAPTER 5: VICES AND VIRTUES — 53

CHAPTER 6: FORGET THE PIPE AND SLIPPERS — 89

CHAPTER 7: A LIFE IN SERVICE — 101

FOREWORD

By the time I retired in 1997, I was the longest-serving Police Drug Squad Officer in the United Kingdom. This can never be surpassed, as Drug Squads have now become Major Crime and Drugs Investigation Units.

I'm immensely proud of that, but there is something that means more to me: if I knew that I had arrested just one young person in possession of drugs and that, as a result, they had reflected on their situation and chosen not to do it again, it would surpass anything else I achieved in my career.

I'll never know for sure, but I very much hope that was the case.

Yaki looking like he had got the cream with Thelma.

CHAPTER 1: FROM SCOUTS TO THE FORCE

To start at the beginning: I was born on the 28th of July in 1948 at a nursing home in Tunbridge Wells, though my parents, Bernard Herbert Brind and Mollie Brind (née Brown), were living in South East London at the time.

My dad had quite a journey during World War II. A surveyor by profession, he had been called up and sent to France but was soon stretchered off at Dunkirk thanks to a bout of appendicitis and ended up in a military hospital in Redcar. During his time there he became engaged to a teacher, but after six months was discharged and sent with the 8th Army to North Africa. Given his skills as a surveyor he was made a gunner, responsible for placing large guns in the right positions with precise elevations.

While in Africa, Dad got a 'Dear John' letter from his fiancée: she was ending their engagement because she'd met someone else. It was during this time that Dad's sister, Betty Brind, asked her friend Mollie Brown to send her brother a Valentine's card to lift his spirits … and that was what brought my parents together and, of course, ultimately meant Clive Brind came to walk the Earth! Dad went on to fight through North Africa and Italy, including the infamous Monte

Cassino, then in 1946, once the war had come to an end, he and Mum married in Eltham, South London.

Dad returned to his pre-war place of work, Thomas & Edge, only to find colleagues who'd not been called to serve during the war were now above him in the company hierarchy. Disheartened, he left to work with James Longley & Co of Crawley, West Sussex. This small building company was to play a big role in constructing several important buildings across the South of England, including the first terminal at Gatwick Airport, Sussex University, and the Brighton Centre. Thanks to Dad's expertise, he became the chief estimator and a director of the company.

Mum was a bit of a funny one. She grew up in a council house in South London, which was bombed out twice in the war. She had four brothers, all 'geezers': one a plumber, one a farmhand, one in the Grenadier Guards and one who called himself a painter … he painted houses! Despite such humble beginnings, Mum had a strong streak of 'Hyacinth Bucket', the snobbish comedy TV character, in her. She loved to hold 'Drinky Parties' and always thought she was above most people. She was not the most loving of mothers, but she was mine. Once Mum married my dad, she never worked again. He was very good to her.

In 1952, we left our small bungalow, which was so close to Gatwick Airport that the windows shook every time a plane flew over, and moved to a house in Northgate in Crawley, opposite what was to become my infant and primary school. The following year, my brother Stephen was born, and our family was complete.

GET YOUR COAT, YOU'RE NICKED!

At the age of eight I did something which played a big part in deciding the path I was to follow in life: I joined the 1st Crawley Cubs. This led to joining the 1st Crawley Scouts (the first in Sussex; we even had the original 'Canadian Mounty' style hats with brims that needed sugar water to keep them in shape) and meeting Cy Barnett, an excellent Scout Master and wonderful guy who made a huge impression on me. He was younger than most adults there yet an exceptional leader, and I really thought he was The Man; in fact, in later years, I was very glad to be able to contact Cy's son and, through him, extend my gratitude.

I loved the scouting life of camping and adventures, learning first aid and self-reliance and being part of a team. Eventually, we moved ten miles away to Hayward's Heath, and I moved to the Third Haywards Heath Scout Troop, where, as the only First Class Scout, I was made Troop Leader and given my third stripe. I then moved to the Senior Scouts at the First Haywards Heath but eventually went back to the Third, only this time as temporary Scout Leader. It took months for a new leader to be appointed, but when he finally arrived, I didn't think he was particularly competent – and he didn't like me a whole lot either. Unfortunately, we fell out, and I left scouting for good. Despite that, I always look back and thank the movement for giving me a great grounding in life.

While still in education, there was another incident that left a lasting impression and had a big impact on my career choice. Walking to school one morning, a young girl ran across the road in front of me – but hadn't seen a car approaching.

She was tossed up in the air before landing heavily on the road in front of me, and I ran to help. I took off my coat, laid it over her, and tried to keep her as comfortable as possible while we waited for an ambulance to arrive. Thankfully, she recovered, but I had to make a statement to the police. Later that day, I was called into the Headmaster's office, where he congratulated me on my actions, and I also received a 'Thankyou' from the girl's mum. My own mum, however, ever the Hyacinth Bucket, grumbled about having to get my bloodstained coat dry cleaned, though I'm sure she was proud of me too.

School itself was … OK. When we'd moved to Haywards Heath, I'd been about to start my final year, so I decided to continue where I was, at Hazelwick in Crawley. My academic achievements weren't much to write home about (I eventually achieved six UEIs, the precursor to CSEs), but that didn't matter: by that time, I knew exactly what I wanted to do with my life.

In June 1964, I applied to join the Police Cadets, starting with the Metropolitan Police. I didn't get in, but I was determined, so next, I tried East Sussex Constabulary. That application led me to take an entrance exam at Lewes Police HQ, where I struck up a conversation with a fellow candidate called Tim Carter, but on that attempt, I also failed to get in. Next was Chichester HQ for the entrance exam for West Sussex Constabulary – and who should I bump into but Tim! That time, we both passed and following an interview, we were both accepted, subject to the medical. As far as I was concerned, I was in – and over the moon!

The day of the medical arrived, and I was called in to see the doctor, who turned out to be 85 if he was a day, almost certainly long-retired and probably just summoned out of his armchair on occasional days such as these. He asked me a few questions about my health, tested my eyesight by means of the memorable, 'What colour is this red pencil?', and put me through the standard eye test of those days, reading letters from a card a short distance away.

A few days later, I received a letter from the West Sussex Chief Constable telling me I'd failed to get in as I'd not passed the sight test. To say I was shocked is an understatement; in fact, it still amazes me today, given that at 75 years old, I still only wear glasses occasionally. But back then, I was devastated. I'd come so close to achieving my ambition, only to have it seemingly taken away for nonsense.

I had no choice but to return to school and, for a few weeks, dragged myself in with no idea as to what I was going to do next. And then it was announced: the Chief Constable of West Sussex, then Mr T C Williams, was doing a tour of the area's schools to promote policing as a career. I attended of course, and so did my dad, who waited behind after for a chat with the Chief. Dad told him what had happened and – having explained he was on good terms with Sir Norman Longley, his employer and the senior officer of West Sussex Constabulary, who would provide me with a reference – the Chief agreed to look into the matter.

Ten days later a letter addressed to me and bearing the West Sussex Constabulary crest dropped through the letterbox. With shaking hands, I opened the envelope and unfolded the letter. It was great news. I was in – subject to no further deterioration in my eyesight, a clause I believe I have dutifully fulfilled!

I was on the path to a career in policing and a fulfilling life of service thanks to Scouting, some chance encounters, perseverance – and good old Dad.

Yaki at school in Crawley (not so studious).

Yaki in West Sussex Constabulary Cadet uniform in 1964.

Clive, Alex Bun, Peter Morgan, Peter Dawson
Robert Comolli & Bob Batey
1962.

Yaki's 14th birthday party with his best mates and Bob Batey, far right.

CHAPTER 2: NEWLY HATCHED

In October 1964, as a newly hatched Police Cadet, I walked through the doors of the Police Station at Shoreham-by-Sea – and the first person I set eyes on was my new friend Tim Carter. It was a nice surprise to find he'd been posted there, too; as it turned out, our paths would cross many times over our careers, and we remained close friends throughout.

My duties as a Cadet were numerous and varied. One day, I could be covering an absent Lollipop Lady on a school crossing, though thankfully, I wasn't made to wear her white coat. Other times, I would be given a beaten-up police cycle and told to cover Southwick beat, about two miles from the nick. Like every beat, Southwick had a number of telephone kiosks, and on the hour and half-hour, you had to stand by the kiosk so if required the station could phone to give you instructions. There were no personal radios in those days.

Some days, however, brought the more ... unexpected. One of my first jobs at Shoreham was to go with PC Walter Weatherley to the mortuary at Southlands Hospital. Walt was the Coroner's Officer who dealt with all sudden deaths, and we were required to identify a body that had been found in the streets of Shoreham. How we were going to identify him I had no idea. I was 16 years old and very wet behind the ears.

Once at the mortuary, the attendant went to a large wall of drawers and pulled out a tray with a dead male on it. Walt got out his ink pad and paper squares, ready to take fingerprints. I simply stood by, watching; I had no idea what was going to happen next.

'Right then, hold out his hand,' said Walt. I steeled myself and reached for the right fist, its fingers clenched, trying not to shudder as, for the first time, I felt the cold waxiness of lifeless skin. 'Open his fingers out,' he instructed. I tried the thumb and then the forefinger, but they were stiff as a … stiff. Rigor mortis had set in. 'I can't,' I said, 'They're rigid.'

His reply? 'Well, you're going to have to break 'em then.' You can imagine my horror as I broke each finger so Walter could ink the body's fingers and place each on the paper square. I vividly remember thinking at that moment about my old schoolmates who were probably playing football in the playground. I could see I was going to have to grow up quickly.

Another momentous thing happened in those early weeks at Shoreham: 'Yaki' came into being. It was December, and the annual Kids' Christmas Party was coming up, meaning entertainment was required. And as often happens in these matters, the job was passed down the ranks: the Superintendent phones the Chief Inspector, who phones the Inspector, who phones the Sergeant, who turns to us Cadets: 'You boys are going to have to do something.'

I was the last in, meaning my rank was alongside the Station Cat, who was not good at performing at the best of times, but then again, nor was I. But nominated I was. I was required to put on a show in front of the invited audience of Police Officers and all their children ... which was pretty daunting. I had no idea what I could do.

That day, I had to cover a school crossing patrol in the town centre. En route, I passed the local Woolworths – and did a double take. It was running a pre-Christmas toy campaign selling glove puppets. Well, I thought, that looks promising. I went in, asked to speak to the manager and told him my dilemma – throwing in a good amount of 'new, well-meaning Police Cadet' and 'well-deserving children at Christmas' for good measure. He must have felt suitably sorry for me because he said I could borrow a puppet and bring it back after the performance for no charge. I had to think of a name to call this glove puppet, and 'Yaki the Duck' was born.

After a bit of practice, I'd perfected (well, it was ok) a comedy duck voice, and on the day performed a passable ventriloquist act, which went down pretty well. From that day on, I was known to all at work as Yaki, including when I retired and went to American Express – and that's still my name to old colleagues to this day. Having an unusual name came to stand me in good stead, particularly in the CID and Drug Squad with informants, as there was always more than one Dave, John and Tim in the department ... but there was only ever one Yaki.

Soon, I was given the job of CID Cadet, which meant I had to record every crime in the division. This was a matter of recording factual details in ledgers – there were no computers yet, of course. It was a mundane task but broken up by the monthly visits to HQ in Chichester for training in criminal law, self-defence and drill, as well as weekly visits to Worthing College for lessons in the British constitution, English and, believe it or not, typing.

Every week, my fellow Cadets and I would meet at Worthing Police Station, where a guy called Don McCloud would be waiting in his Lancaster van. This van had seen better days, plus the base of the van was made of wood, and the weight of us in the back caused the tyres to rub against the floor, but it was better than walking, so we'd all pile in. Inevitably, about a mile after setting off, the smell of burning wood and rubber would hit our noses, but beggars couldn't be choosers.

Once at the college, we all looked forward to the typing lesson for one reason only: there were girls in the class, which brought out the show-off in some. Sometimes, we had to put on headphones and type in time with the music. Then periodically, a voice would come over the track to say, 'Carriage Return,' which was our cue to push the carriage return bar. One memorable day, I was sitting behind a Cadet called Stuart Johnson, who was a bit of a character. When the words 'Carriage Return' came over the headphones, he returned a bit too enthusiastically, and the carriage left his typewriter, seemed to hover in the aisle between the seats for a moment, then fell to the floor with a resounding crash. You can imagine the sight of fifteen teenage boys trying to suppress their laughter; we weren't very successful.

In late 1965, I was posted to Chichester with accommodation in the Section House. My room was about 12ft by 10ft, with a cupboard and a set of drawers, and apart from a communal canteen, that was it. But to me, it was great, and I was happy to be away from home and free.

I'd been posted to the Operations Room, the hub of the Force, where we took 999 calls and, via radio, directed cars around the county. I worked alongside a police constable and a police sergeant, and an inspector was there most of the time. My role was the same as theirs, with the added burden of covering the switchboard when the telephonist clocked off. The idea was that we had to switch the alarm on when she left so we could be notified when a call was coming in. A great idea in theory – but in reality, it didn't always get switched on, and if you happened to pass the switchboard during the night, it wasn't unknown for it to be lit up like Blackpool Illuminations with some rather irate callers waiting to be spoken to.

Broadcasting over the airwaves to my colleagues was daunting at first. I got used to it, but the memory of one incident still makes me chuckle. A car had been stolen from Bognor, and it was down to me to circulate its details. I started well with the standard format: 'Stolen today from Bognor, a Blue Ford Anglia registration number 457,' but when it came to the rest of the registration and, more specifically, my retention of the phonetic alphabet, things went downhill: 'A Alpha, B Bravo, K ... K... Canary.' I think the collective laughter from every Police Station and Police Car around the County could probably be heard from Hampshire. A few choice comments came back over the airwaves, too.

That wasn't my only slip-up. When on nights, we had to carry out name and date of birth checks on behalf of Officers out in the field. As the Force Intelligence Room was only covered in the day I would need to go through the SUSCRO index cards looking for details. Most checks came back negative, which required the radio message back to the Officer: 'With regard to your search, no trace, over.' I would say this many times in an eight-hour shift. But a slip is never too far away, and one night, I replied to one Officer, 'Re your trace, no search, over.' Again, I received a number of well-deserved caustic responses.

Life in the Section House had its laughs, too. Most of my fellow residents were PCs, though a number were slightly older than me, such as Paul 'Dusty' Miller, an ex-Cadet and very nice guy – but that didn't stop us when one night we decided to play a prank on him. He was on night shift and patrolling Chichester city centre when, at about 1 a.m., five of us left the Section House with a handful of light bulbs and a childish plan. Knowing the city centre was linked by terraced buildings, we made our way along the rooftops until we spotted Dusty doing what cops did in those days: checking the doors of the shops to ensure security. One of our little team snuck a little closer and then dropped a light bulb to the ground. We expected the resulting 'Pop!' and smash would cause Dusty to go and investigate … but to our horror, he dived into a nearby telephone box and dialled 999, evidently unwilling (probably sensibly!) to investigate a burglary-in-progress single-handed. We were given a talking-to in the house the next morning, but nothing serious came of it, luckily for us.

GET YOUR COAT, YOU'RE NICKED!

Cadet life was necessarily varied, and in the early part of 1967, I had to perform three months of Community Service. For some reason, I chose to go to an Approved School for in the middle of nowhere, in South Darrenth on the outskirts of Dartford in South London. I didn't drive and had no way of going anywhere during any downtime, although it quickly transpired that there wasn't to be much anyway.

On arrival, I was sent to the office to read up on the inmates' files and convictions. They didn't make for happy reading. Most were East End London kids, and most of them had broken home lives plus convictions that made for hair-raising reading. One lad who I came to quite like was 14 and small for his age at about four feet ten: his most recent conviction had been for taking and driving away a double-decker bus. I still don't know how he reached the pedals.

The next day, I rose bright and early, ready to get started but a little apprehensive at what was ahead, to be told I was to take a group on the sports field for baseball. Ever the good Cadet, I didn't question whether it was a good idea to give pupils at this particular school a baseball bat and tell them their PTI was in the Police – and sure enough, the first time I gave a lad 'Out,' he came running at me with the bat raised above his head, ready to take my head off. By a stroke of luck, I managed to duck under the bat, grab his wrist and throw him over my shoulder. As he lay on the ground, I grabbed the bat out of his hand, pointed it down at his throat and said, 'Now, you won't do that again, will you?'

It was a fine moment as there were about 25 other boys in the field who saw the incident, though I have to admit if he had done it again, I very possibly wouldn't have been so lucky, and he might have made a large dent in my head. Nonetheless, I was pretty chuffed I'd made the impression I had, and I didn't have too much trouble after that.

As the weeks went by, I came to understand a bit more about the boys and what some of them were up against. They were sent to the school for a minimum of nine months to up to about three years, but to some degree, how long they would serve was up to them. At first, they were allocated a Grade seven and then assessed monthly: if all was OK, they were upgraded until they got to Grade One, then RA, which stood for Responsible Adult and indicated imminent 'release'.

At first, I struggled to understand why some boys would get to their second month in RA and within touching distance of going home only to 'do a runner', get arrested and then returned both to the school and Grade seven. Over time, I concluded that, for them, life was better in the Approved School than at home. There, they had activities, three good meals a day, and no worries.

Those three months were rewarding but intense. My working day started at 8 a.m. and finished at lights out at 10 p.m. and I only had Sundays off. The only bit of time out I managed was with another guy, a university student on release; at 10 p.m. on the dot, we would head out and run the ½ mile to the only pub in Darrenth to catch last orders and one solitary but delicious pint at 10.30 p.m.

One memory from that time still makes me smile. Mum and Dad came to visit one Sunday after I'd been there for about six weeks but got lost on the way. Lost in some backwater, Dad had to pull over, and Mum had to wind down her window to ask for directions: 'To South Darrenth Approved School.' I can just imagine her face, and it still makes me laugh to this day.

After three months, I returned to Chichester to complete my Cadet service. What's more, as I'd now reached the age of 19, I was eligible to apply to Training School and potentially join the Police Force as a fully-fledged officer. But before any of that could happen, I had to attend the Assistant Chief Constable's Office for an interview and to be told which Training School I would be going to.

On the day of the interview, I sat outside the office alongside a guy called Phil Johnson, who was waiting for the same. I was a little nervous, not about anything in particular, but the ACC, Mr Tiplady, was a high-ranking officer, and this was a bit of a landmark moment. My name was called first, and I stood slowly. I straightened out my uniform, took a deep breath, walked into the office and saluted ... only to receive the biggest bollocking of my life.

He wanted to know why I thought I should be allowed to go on to Training School and why I thought I was worthy of becoming a police officer. He picked through my record so far, noting every misdemeanour, every less-than-perfect grade. He spoke for quite a few minutes about the time when I and a fellow cadet had covered another lad's car in mud, prompting his father to put in a complaint. And finally, he wondered out loud what the hell he ought to do with me.

The bollocking only ended when Tiplady told me to get out of his office and wait in the corridor while he decided if I was going to be allowed to continue in the Police. I emerged back in the waiting room, no doubt a little pale and sweaty, and told Phil what had happened. He was called in next – and got the same barrage as me. When he came out, he told me he thought he wouldn't be allowed in either. We were then both called back into the office only to be told by the ACC that he was going to give us a last chance and we would be going to Sandgate in Kent. To this day, I don't know why any of that occurred. Perhaps it was a scare tactic designed to keep us on our toes … and it probably worked, for a while at least.

In August 1967, I began my 13-week Basic Police Training at Sandgate Training Centre in Folkestone, Kent, under the guidance of Sergeant Paylor, a brilliant tutor and all-around good man. The Training Centre was a formidable building, and we were taught Basic Police Training, which included criminal law, PE, drill, and all aspects of policing, including practical scenarios.

The training was residential from Monday to Friday, and we stayed in dormitories with about ten of us in each room – so inevitably, some mucking about took place. One night, I – a sensible, reliable, soon-to-be Police Officer – was fully engaged in a vicious pillow fight when I fell onto a lamp and got a large gash on my shoulder. The blood just wouldn't stop, so the Duty Sergeant was alerted, and he carted me off to A&E. The nurse who attended me declared that the wound needed stitches and offered the option of waiting for a doctor to anaesthetize the area, or she could just put the stitches in there and then. The Sergeant's growled reply?

'He's a "rufty tufty" policeman. Just put the stitches in.' She did just that, and I guess it served me right.

I ploughed on through the course, just about passing the monthly exams. I started well, coming seventh out of 75 on the first exam, but I took my foot off the gas and went down the list until just scraping through the last.

Finally, the end of training and a career in law enforcement was in sight, with just the formal Passing Out Parade to go. Crowds of relatives were there, including my mum and dad, dressed in their finest, all gathered to see the marching display of those who had completed the course, and again, it's a comment of Mum's I remember most from that day. As the tallest, I was right-hand marker, which meant that when marching I had to keep my eyes front at all times so as not to deviate from the march past. Specifically, this meant that when the command 'Eyes right' was shouted out, I did as I was instructed to do – only to hear my mum's distinctive voice cry out, 'Oh no, Clive hasn't turned his head!' Yet another embarrassing moment for her, but an amusing one for me!

So that was it. I had achieved the aim that I had been dreaming of and working towards since I was fourteen. I was a qualified Police Officer, and a whole new world was about to open up.

Sandgate Training School 1967, Yaki at centre back.

CHAPTER 3: A JOURNEY IN BLUE

P roudly, I stood, pristine in my perfectly pressed black suit, silver buttons and black boots shining. It was December 1967, and I was just starting a night shift as I was now an official member of 'The Force.'

Two months previously, West Sussex Constabulary had posted me to Bognor Regis, and I'd found digs in the town with a couple of guys, Mick Clarke and Phill Hall, who were to become good mates. Thanks to my dad, I even had my own car. I was nineteen years old, and life seemed good. Little did I know that in a matter of hours, I would encounter what I still consider to be one of the most traumatic incidents in my life.

That evening was a cold one, but with Christmas just around the corner, spirits were high, so I didn't mind setting out into the chill to drop off some road signs in the only vehicle Bognor Police had at that time, a dark blue Dormobile van. Job done. I was heading back to the old Bognor Police Station when a call came in over my personal radio: there had been a road traffic accident just outside Bognor on Chichester Road. As the only police officer out in a vehicle, it was all up to me.

The scene I arrived at shook me to my core, and the memory of it still haunts me to this day. The skies were pitch black as all the street lights were out by that time of night. All

I had to see by was the revolving blue lamp on the top of my van. That allowed me to see that two vehicles had collided head-on, and seven young people, all around my age, were strewn across the road.

Two were clearly dead, and I could do nothing for them. Despite my shock at what I was seeing, I was able to think clearly and knew my priority was the living, all of whom were badly injured. The first thing I did was summon an ambulance, though I knew, as it was the only one in Bognor with a driver on call from home, it wouldn't be with me any time soon.

Shortly after I arrived, a coachload of rugby players on their way home from a festive fancy-dress party pulled up, and some of them were able to help comfort and warm the crash victims. There I was, still wet behind the ears at 19 years old, with two bodies and five seriously injured, in a scene lit only by a rotating blue light and made even more surreal by the various fancy dress costumes. As the only Police Officer, all eyes were on me. Having been a Cadet since the age of 16, I may have seen and experienced more than my old school friends, but I was still very new and learning on the job.

It felt like an eternity before the ambulance arrived, followed not long after by a Traffic Police car. I pointed out the most seriously injured, and the ambulance took off with two on stretchers and one walking wounded. I stayed behind with the rest and focussed on a young lady who was trapped by her legs in one of the cars. I spoke to her and comforted her while her head rested on my lap, though she was drifting in and out of consciousness. Eventually, we were able to extract her from the mangled car and, once it had returned, place her in the ambulance. As it sped off Chichester Hospital, I breathed a sigh of relief. I had done my best, and she was on her way to proper medical care.

Sadly, I learned later she had died in the back of the ambulance before she reached the hospital. I was the last person she had spoken to.

For a long time afterwards, I was haunted by questions. Was I to blame? Had I made the wrong decision? Should she have gone to the hospital first?

Of course, those questions remained unanswered, which is as hard to accept now as it was then. But I do know I tried my best. Every police officer swore an oath to save lives, and I tried. Yet, to this day, I still shed a tear when remembering that night.

Not long after, I found myself on another night shift in Bognor Town Centre, which also turned out to be eventful. At around 2 a.m. I got a personal radio call telling me to go to a lady who had reported her husband missing. It didn't seem like an urgent call, but I started up my Panda car and made my way over to where she was about four miles away in Barnham. As I passed the Railway Station there, I spotted a lady in the middle of the road, waving her arms. I hopped out and went on over. 'I gather you want to report your husband missing, Madam,' I said, getting my pocketbook out.

'Oh yes,' she said. 'He went over there behind that hedge 'cos he needed a pee, but he ain't come back!'

My face must have been a picture – but duty called. I hurried over to look behind 'that hedge' only to see a very low wall, behind which the earth dropped away to a low-down stream ... and there was the husband, upside down with his nose just an inch or two above the water line. I scrambled down to him, but in doing so, my transmitter fell out of my jacket and plopped into the water. I was totally by myself and now had no good way of raising help. I managed to turn the man over so he didn't drown, but there was no way I was going to get him out by myself. I started yelling for help and was somewhat surprised when the wife didn't show herself – or perhaps I shouldn't have been, as she'd shown a distinct lack of curiosity thus far. She eventually heard and flagged down a car then, with the help of the driver and his tow rope, I managed to haul the man up to dry land. It was a dramatic rescue that could easily have gone awry, and the man had been very lucky – though neither he nor his good lady wife saw fit to say even a small 'thanks' at the end. Not a dickie bird.

In those days, it seemed the strangest incidents happened during the hours of darkness. Late one night, I was walking through Bognor's empty streets, the eerie silence broken only by the impending arrival of the milkman, when I spotted a movement under a car. I went to investigate only for a young man to come scrambling out and go sprinting off down the road. I had no idea what he'd done, but clearly, it was something he didn't want me finding out about, so I set off on his tail. The lad was very fast and determined not to be caught, but I put on a spurt, grabbed him, and we ended up wrestling on the ground. Eventually, I managed to apprehend him and dragged him into the nick, where he was charged with assaulting a police officer and stealing a car.

When he was later interviewed, it was discovered that he was a deserter from the Army trying to evade capture. When he eventually came before the Court, the Magistrate handed the lad a fine for his crimes and expressed hope for his military career – but made no mention of the impact there could have been on my own career had he done me some damage during our fight.

Life at work was busy, sometimes thrilling and sometimes less so, as being pretty much bottom ranking meant the crappy jobs would often land in my lap. But that was okay – I was learning a lot, and life outside of work was pretty good, too. I was playing football for the Force at a pretty high level, and when I wasn't doing that, I could often be found with my mates having a few beers in the town's nightclubs, particularly one called The Bali Hai … where one night I got chatting to a young woman who I thought was just lovely.

I already knew her a little: her name was Thelma, and she'd been going out with a mate of mine who'd then joined the Merchant Navy. She wanted to know when he was going to be back, but I (seeing as though my mate clearly wasn't that keen) was more interested in getting her to dance with me. She eventually agreed, and at the end of the night, I asked if I could see her again. She took a bit of persuasion, but again, I won her round in the end … and the rest, as they say, is history. After about six weeks, I knew she was The One for me and asked her to marry me. Thankfully, I didn't need to persuade her on that one!

Following two years probation as a PC on the beat, in December 1970, I was assigned an Aide to CID, which involved learning the ropes of being a detective. Not much happened during that three-month stint; as an Aide, you'd still get crappy jobs such as theft from fruit machines.

But then, in February 1971, I was told I was being posted to Brighton. This was a shock, as Thelma and I had just got engaged and the wedding was set for April 10th. After some negotiations, the posting was delayed until after the wedding … the very next day after, in fact.

We had a lot of planning yet to do. Lots of family members and friends were invited and my best man was to be Bob Batey, a guy who was already important to me and who would continue to be so for a long time to come.

Our wedding day dawned, and despite the impending move, we had a lovely day. The ceremony was held in the church in Yapton where Thelma had grown up and was followed by a reception in a lovely hotel in Barnham, which happened to be right next to the stream from which I had rescued the 'missing' husband, though thankfully I managed to stay dry on that day.

After the reception, Thelma and I got into our car and set off for Brighton, where our police flat, our first home together, was waiting. We were excited as well as inevitably a little nervous at what awaited us as we set out on our new life together.

GET YOUR COAT, YOU'RE NICKED!

Little did we know that a rather unpleasant surprise would come knocking on our door the very next morning.

Bognor CID football team, Yaki back second from left and his old mate Bob Batey third from left.

CHAPTER 4: RIGHTING WRONGS

The sun was barely rising on the morning after our wedding when we were abruptly woken by an insistent knocking on our flat door. We stumbled to open it only to find a Detective Chief Inspector and a Detective Sergeant, who asked if they could come in.

They had a question for us – had we seen our neighbour, as they were hopeful he might be able to 'help them with some ongoing enquiries'? We replied that we hadn't, as we'd only moved in the night before and hadn't met a soul yet. Thelma found them some paper (as it happened, this was from a writing set that was a wedding gift from the day before), the DS jotted down a note and thanked us for our cooperation, and they left us wondering about the true nature of our new neighbours.

It was an unsettling start to our married and my working life in Brighton. In the days that followed, the full extent of what had happened came to light. A number of Brighton police officers had been caught red-handed, pilfering from parked cars and shops while on night shifts – including the local Dorothy Perkins branch where Thelma was due to start work that week. The very people who should have been protecting the city had been the ones undermining its safety.

After an investigation, nine officers were prosecuted for their involvement in criminal activities, which included theft from unattended motor vehicles and robberies from local stores. They'd stolen front window keys for shops like Dorothy Perkins and Burtons, gaining easy access to items they then sold. We heard that one of our neighbours had pilfered a leather jacket from Burton's window and brought it home, telling his wife she needn't buy him a birthday present as he'd already done it himself – and so she could just give him the money!

Even those who were not directly involved copped it. One Officer, who bought an evidently dodgy radio off of one of the guys involved, decided to throw it off Brighton Pier and into the sea – but he was found out and dismissed.

The ripples spread wide. One guy bought a car from one of those involved but then felt there could be something iffy about it, so he told CID about his concerns. When they took a look at it, they found everything in it, including the wheels, were all stolen. As he'd put his hand up to it, he escaped any allegations of wrongdoing.

The consequences for those that had been involved were severe – our neighbour and others were dismissed from the force, convicted and carted off to prison. The families of those in police accommodation inevitably lost their homes, too.

That wasn't all. The news of what these Officers had done was splashed across the local press, and the rest of us were exposed to ridicule and suspicion from the public. Everywhere we Police Officers went, people pointed fingers and made snide remarks. Sussex Police themselves were, at that time, running a campaign called 'Catch a Thief' and had posters showing a man in a black and white shirt and mask running away with a swag bag – and police helmets got drawn on to the thief. Even Thelma copped some flack ... imagine her response on her first day at work in Dorothy Perkins when she was asked, 'What does your husband do?'

Within the force, everyone was looking over their shoulder, especially the Sergeants who were severely criticized for failing to adequately supervise the offending Officers. I felt the effects for sure – on my first week of nights, I had my pocketbook signed (the system in place for senior officers to check junior officers' actions) 28 times in a week when usually it would have been once or twice, if that. It seemed on every corner, there was a Sergeant with a pen.

I copped some personal flack of my own care of my new Chief Superintendent – a guy called, funnily enough, 'Yaki' Rostrom. In the early days of my new start in Brighton I had been told to go to his office for an introductory meeting.

This was pretty standard and not too daunting as by then, I'd been in the job for four years – seven if you include my time as a Cadet – and I was a police driver. I thought I was just going to get a ' Welcome to the Division' chat and perhaps a lecture about 'How things are done around here,' maybe with an edge to keep me on my toes considering the ongoing scandal. I was not expecting to get the second biggest bollocking of my life.

I knocked on his door and entered the room as smartly and respectfully as required. So far, so good. 'I want to see your pocketbook,' he said. I passed it over, and he roughly leafed through then threw it back at me. 'There's been nothing put in it for three months,' he snapped, glaring at me.

I was surprised. 'No Sir,' I explained, 'I've just come from being a CID Aide.' Surely, he knew that was to be expected: as a CID Officer, you didn't write in a pocketbook; you wrote in a desk diary, which stayed on division.

He wasn't happy but turned his attention to my cap, looking at it as if it had just said something rude about his mum. 'Look at your cap,' he said. 'Have you doctored it?'

I had to admit he had me there. It was just one of those things: the peaks of our caps used to stand straight out, but we thought they looked better if they pointed down a little, like a Guardsman, so we'd bend them a little on either side.

I cleared my throat. 'Just a little bit, Sir.'

'Well, you can get that changed at the stores straight away,' he growled.

'Oh yes, sir. Thank you.' Was he finished? I just wanted to go.

'And by the way,' he continued, 'don't think you'll be going anywhere near a car for the next three months.' He really seemed to have taken a dislike to me. I just wanted to get out and keep my head down until he forgot I existed.

'Yes, Sir.' I went to leave, but it turned out he had one last thing to comment on.

'By the way, I understand you and I might have the same nickname.'

'Yes Sir,' I nodded, not sure where this was going. He was, and still is, the only other 'Yaki' I'd ever met, though he came about because he was Welsh (I'm guessing something to do with the Welsh for Cheers! being iechyd, pronounced yaki, da!).

He smirked. 'I don't think anyone's going to get us confused, do you?!'

'No, Sir,' I said, slipping out the door as fast as I could. Exit stage left!

Despite his warning, I was driving a police vehicle within three days, thanks to a shortage of manpower, and eventually put on North General Patrol Car. The vehicle allocated for this was an Austin Westminster, a big old bus with blue lights and two-tone horns. In those days, I didn't go into the Police Station much as Brighton had Police Boxes, each with a phone connected to Brighton's switchboard, dotted around the whole division. These were basic (and certainly not as good as Doctor Who's), although some town centre ones were okay. In fact, the one next to Brighton Palace Pier was made up of two rooms, one used as a holding area for a prisoner and the other containing a desk and tea-making facilities.

The Box I reported to was on the Main London to Brighton road about three miles north of the town, and the GP car was always parked in a small layby about 25 yards from the box. One night, I was heading in for duty and, as usual, first went into the Police Box to grab everything I needed, then walked back to the GP car, taking a shortcut over a patch of recently cut grass. I started up the engine and was sitting waiting to turn onto the main road when suddenly my foot slipped off the clutch, and the car lurched forward – smacking into the rear of the car in front.

I was so embarrassed. I got out and explained to the driver of the car I'd hit that it had been my error, but we'd have to wait for a Supervisory Officer to come and take the details of the accident. With reddening cheeks I radioed in.

My section mate Tony Crawford was Acting Sergeant at the time, and it was he who arrived to take down all the details. He reported me for careless driving, which was standard, though very happily for me, it was decided no further action would be taken. Happily for Tony, it turned out his decision to report me (for which I never took offence: he was doing his duty) helped get him promoted to Sergeant not long after. Not a great night for me but – hey, it could have been worse, and it worked out well for Tony!

Not long after that incident, and at a time when the police corruption scandal was still casting a shadow, I was driving down the main London to Brighton road when I spotted a Rolls Royce in front, swerving all over the road. I decided to pull the driver over.

Obediently, he stopped the car, and when I approached the open driver's side window, I was unsurprised to smell alcohol fumes. 'You've been drinking,' I said. 'I'm going to have to give you a breath test,' I said. He followed me to my car, protesting his innocence.

He sat in the passenger seat of my panda car, and I prepared the test, which in those days consisted of glass vials and various coloured liquids. I gave him the breath test, and as I did so, he pressed something into my left hand. I looked down, and he slipped me a ten-pound note, which in those days was a whole week's wages.

I can honestly say for not one second was I tempted to keep that money. Immediately, I did as I had been taught and squiggled my signature on it.

This had all happened in a very short period – and we'd not had the result of the breath test yet. I held the vial up to the light ... and it was negative. Nonetheless, I nicked him for attempted bribery. This was literally just months after the crimes of those Brighton police officers had been exposed, and I was happy to be able to demonstrate that not all cops are bad. The Rolls Royce driver, though not guilty of drunk driving, later appeared in court and was fined very heavily for attempting to bribe a police officer.

Later that year, I moved to the Plain Clothes Unit, or 'Vice Squad', and was now out of uniform. The squad was newly formed and had been created out of a need to clean up Brighton's increasingly grubby reputation for being a place where public sex and other unsavoury activities were rife. We were tasked with flushing out the 'dirty raincoat brigade', men who took part in sexual activity in public places such as toilets and alleyways, as well as dealing with vulnerable young prostitutes and monitoring the activities of the area's many sex shops.

One job I recall from this time involved carrying out test purchases at bookshops, and in particular, one on Sydney Street, to ensure they weren't selling illegal pornography. There was an added element to this job, however, as there were suspicions that a serving Police Officer may have been illicitly involved in one of these shops, and we were again warned to be on the lookout for any signs of police corruption.

Just a couple of days after being told this, I was in the process of booking in a prisoner at Brighton cell block when the jailer, a guy called Tom Dyer, pulled me to one side. He wanted to ask me something: were we planning on carrying out any test purchases in Sydney Street? None that I was aware of, I said. He then went on to say that if our team was going to do one it would be worth my while letting him know.

It was disappointing. Tom was an officer getting towards the end of his Policing career, and I'd known him for many years, but I was not going to be compromised. I immediately reported what had been said and discovered Tom had already been under suspicion and the subject of background financial checks. I was just confirming what had already been thought. It came as no surprise when, later that week, Tom suddenly retired, just a little short of 30 years and therefore on a reduced pension.

Despite the unpleasant nature of much of my working day, life at home with Thelma was very good and much more wholesome! By now, we had managed to buy our first property, a small bungalow in Greenfield Crescent in Brighton, and then in March 1974, our son Gary was born.

Professionally, I was always keen to keep moving, learning and gaining experience, and after a couple of years, I again took on an Aide to CID role at a time when two very big cases, the Black Lion murder and the Royal Albion fire, were taking up lots of police time. There was just a Detective Sergeant, Detective Constable, and me left on division dealing with everything else, and it was a highly pressurised time; for the first time in my career, I took work home and lay awake at night worrying about everything I hadn't managed to find time to do yet.

Despite this, after three months, I interviewed for Brighton CID and was accepted, but there were no vacancies, so as a stopgap, I decided to join Sussex Drug Squad ... little knowing that 20 years later, I'd still be there.

From the start, I enjoyed the work and was able to leverage some of the intelligence and contacts from my days on Vice. I'd got to know the managers and owners of some of Brighton's gay clubs and one evening, I got a call from one who was worried someone may have been dealing drugs in his club. He asked me to pop in for a chat, so I set off with Mick Cooper, my wingman at the time, who hadn't had much experience with the more flamboyant elements of the town's nightlife.

The club was in the basement of the Brighton Esplanade Hotel. We headed down the steps, and the doorman took us through the dimly lit club to the manager. He was in the middle of dealing with something, so he hurried off, telling us to get some drinks.

Mick and I sidled off to the bar. 'Yes, darling, what can I get you?' asked the barman. I could see Mick wasn't comfortable, but the barman's camp manner didn't bother me. I mustered the deepest voice I could, ordered a couple of pints, and then Mick and I turned to face the rest of the club.

By now, our eyes had adjusted to the gloom, and Mick was able to take in a sight which I had seen before, but he clearly hadn't: a dance floor full of men, some smartly dressed in suits and others in more outrageous outfits, all in various positions of embrace.

The sight of so many men, most of whom were 'romantically entangled', was not one that Mick had experienced before. I have never seen a man down a pint of beer so fast. Mick drained the last drop, turned to me and said, 'You're on your own on this one, Yak,' then virtually ran out of the club. I was kind enough to go and find him later.

Being on the Drug Squad often meant being in places where looking like an officer would mean you stuck out like a sore thumb, so it made sense to try and blend in. During the notoriously hot summer of 1976, my normal attire was a pair of jeans and a denim waistcoat, which went well with my long, curly brown hair and beard. During the winter, I wore what was known as an 'Afghan' coat, a thick sheepskin number with a big fluffy collar, and my partner Tony Baker wore a big black 'Cromby', which made him look a little menacing, so we weren't the most conventional looking pair.

Dressed like this, at the end of a 2 p.m. to 10 p.m. shift, it wasn't unknown for us to visit the Brighton Police Club Bar for a pint before going home. Police Club Bars in those days were great. Most Divisional HQs or large police stations had a bar run by Police Social Committee members or, as in Brighton's case, by a full-time civilian steward. Our bar, like most, was very well stocked and in a great location too, on the top floor of Brighton's Police Station with a panoramic view over the town centre.

One night, we'd just finished our paperwork, so we dashed up to the bar to enjoy a well-earned pint (or two) with a few other Drug Squad colleagues. Before long, we spotted a high-ranking huddle at the other end of the bar: the Chief Constable, the Deputy Chief, an Assistant Chief Constable and the Chief Superintendent of Brighton. We carried on with our pints, but I must have been aware of the group because I saw the Chief turn to one of his group and nod his head in our direction, then heard him mutter, 'Who the hell's that lot over there?' The Chief Superintendent simply replied, 'Oh, that's your Force Drug Squad, Sir!' A smile of relief spread across the Super's face, and then, to his credit, he sauntered over and introduced himself.

In 1977, I had another change of scene when I was detached from the Drug Squad onto a Regional Crime Squad Operation called Operation Yashmack. I was paired with a young Detective Sergeant called Dave Wolsteholme, and we worked out of Seaford Police Station travelling all over the South East carrying out various enquiries into illegal drugs operations. After three months, I was released back to the Drug Squad in Brighton and the operation, under the new name Bentley, later resulted in a large seizure of cannabis in Wales. As fate would have it, many years later, I ended up meeting up with Dave a couple of times, and it was great to catch up and reminisce.

In June of that year, our daughter Sacha was born and we proudly brought her back to our new family home, a semi-detached property on Old Shoreham Road in Southwick. It was wonderful to have our little family complete, though it was 99% down to Thelma to hold the fort at home – and she did a wonderful job.

Family life was just great, and we were very happy in our home – but at work, things were about to go international.

Yaki at his desk in the Drug Squad Office Brighton Police Station.

Sussex Police Drug Squad 1988. Yaki at back far right, Tim Carter front 2nd from right, Tony Baker back 5th from right.

CHAPTER 5: VICES AND VIRTUES

I'd been acting in detective roles for a good while, but in February 1980, it was time to enrol on the official twelve-week residential detective training course. It was good to be finally getting it done, though I'd never been good in a long academic process, and we had a great class of characters, including a DC, Chris Gillings, who had a very good, very dry sense of humour.

One day, we had a lecture from a Senior Prison Officer from Lewes Prison about the searching of prisoners and their visitors. He was telling us about one occasion when a woman had bought a sealed pack of Mr Kipling cakes for her inmate husband, but when the pack was opened and inspected, they found a lump of cannabis under each cake top. Looking very sincere, the Prison Officer went to sum up the 'learning point' for that incident by saying, 'This just goes to prove that', but was cut off by Chris Gillings, who shouted out: 'Mr Kipling makes exceedingly good cakes!' … which, of course, was the brand slogan then as now. The whole class just erupted with laughter.

I met Chris Gillings again a few years later when he was a Uniform Inspector at East Grinstead. As I walked into the office, Dick Duffield was coming on duty as the late Inspector, and Chris was going home, having been the early Inspector, and, as is procedure, the two needed to debrief.

'Anything to report, Inspector?' asked Dick.

'Yes, Inspector,' said Chris. 'It was dark, then it got light.'

Chris got off his seat, Dick Duffield sat down, and the official debriefing was complete. Humour has always been a central part of Police life, and I hope that's still the case today.

The weeks ticked by, the end was nearing, and we were getting a bit de-mob happy. In the final week, each of us had to present a lecture to the class. Mine was about my time as a PTI in the approved school, and then it was the turn of a guy called John Lloyd. He had been brought up in South Africa, and his lecture was on South African Wine. I don't remember much about it, but I do remember he brought in a box of South African wine for all to taste, and of course, the whole class happily tucked in. Nice as it was, the box didn't touch the sides of a class of prospective detectives, so we broke into the wine we'd already bought and set aside for the course finishing party, which was only a week away. The lecture finished with 16 Training Detectives, a Detective Inspector and his two Detective Sergeants all half-pissed in the HQ corridor.

Shortly after the course ended, I was told I had (probably just about) passed the course and was now a fully qualified detective, so I returned to work on the Force Drug Squad in Brighton. The mid-'80s stands out to me as a time when I was working on big cases which sometimes required me to travel abroad, which couldn't have been easy for Thelma at home, keeping everything together and raising Gary and Shacha, who were still small.

GET YOUR COAT, YOU'RE NICKED!

For me, these cases held a degree of excitement. After all, tracking down the bad guys is at the core of what gets every copper through his or her shift, but I was getting to do it (well, sometimes) across countries and sometimes continents.

In 1982, I was the lead detective in a case dealing with an import of cocaine that had arrived in the UK from both Lisbon and Madrid. We needed to obtain evidence from both cities, so my colleague Detective Sergeant Malcolm (Streaky) Bacon and I got on a flight and set off for Lisbon, where we were to spend four days. Once there, our meeting with members of the Lisbon Drug squad wasn't particularly fruitful, so we set about making our own enquiries. We had been allocated one of their detectives to drive us about and translate, and, as was the custom, once work was done, he would help us find places to eat and generally keep us entertained.

On the first evening, this young Detective clearly had no idea where to take us, but eventually, we entered a bar ... which Streaky and I quickly identified as some sort of brothel. As happily married men, this was not quite what we wanted to experience, so we got back in the car, and he drove us to the other extreme: a Fados experience, which is rather highbrow Flamenco. Again, this didn't exactly hit the spot for us, so he gave up and took us to a bar, where we happily spent the rest of the evening and paid for all the drinks.

The next stop was Madrid. Having checked in at our hotel, we headed off to Police HQ, where we were greeted by a couple of Officers. We told them of our need to interview a prisoner who they currently had in custody for drug smuggling and they quickly agreed to get the interview lined up for us for the next day. This wasn't to be a standard set-up: our interviewee was believed to have links to the Mafia, so we could only meet him under strict security conditions, at the most secure court in Madrid.

Happy to have this important step lined up, Streaky and I were headed off, but before we did, we got chatting to the Officers about the football – specifically, the World Cup, which was underway in Madrid. Being the cheeky so-and-sos we were, we asked if there was any chance of getting hold of tickets to the final. The officers laughed along good-naturedly in response, and Streaky and I headed off for the evening and a discussion about how we would approach the interview over a few beers.

We were leaving our hotel the next morning when the concierge called us over and handed me an envelope which apparently had just been dropped in for us. Puzzled, I opened it to find two tickets to the World Cup Final, entirely free. Perhaps we should have wondered how this was arranged … but we were so delighted that we were happy to remain in blissful ignorance on that occasion!

However, we still had work to do. We were taken to the court, where another, far less jovial Spanish Police Force took over, and we were ushered to an underground interview room. The minutes ticked by as we waited, uncomfortable in the stuffy heat, before at last, the heavy door banged open, and the prisoner was marched in by six armed police officers. Even to those who are used to guns, this would be intimidating, but to Streaky and I – who definitely weren't – it was frankly pretty scary. The armed Officers had stationed themselves around the small room, and it felt like they were glowering at us as much as our smuggler friend.

Luckily for us, the prisoner could speak English. He accepted our offer of a cigarette, and our conversation started quite amicably. But after a few questions, that changed: he seemed to have worked out where we had gained our information and ran his finger across his throat with the words, 'Your man is dead.' At least he wasn't threatening us.

As the atmosphere soured, he had been smoking his cigarette down and, in a sudden movement, reached out to the ashtray in the centre of the table to stub it. Immediately, we heard the terrifying 'click' of six safety catches being released – and every gun was trained, if not on us, then a couple of feet away from where we were sitting. There was nowhere to duck or hide. Thankfully, the bullets stayed in their barrels, no guns were fired, and the interview was concluded. We were especially glad to get back to our hotel that night!

We did get to see the Cup Final before we left for home. On a very hot afternoon, Italy beat Germany 3-1, though I have no idea how they played in the stifling heat. Madrid did not sleep that night, though Streaky and I did, following a few beers, of course, as we were keen to get home. We'd had enough excitement for one trip.

Not long after our trip to Madrid, we found ourselves on another cocaine job which centred on Lyon in France. It was agreed that Tim and I would go to Lyon to liaise with their drug squad and customs and to gather evidence, so a couple of days later, we set off, very happy to be flying business class and to avail ourselves of the free drinks. An hour and a half later, we arrived, smiling and 'relaxed', and met up with the Customs Officer we'd come to see – who then invited us to go for a drink. We were only too happy to accept.

As is probably evident by now, I'll drink most things – but pastis was new to me. It's an alcoholic (and, as I was to discover, very potent) anise-flavoured apéritif which needs to be watered down, after which it looks milky and pretty harmless. I'm usually quite good at knowing my limit (you can see where this is going), but because I didn't know the strength of this drink or how much I had consumed, after a short time in the bar with the customs officer, I believe I may have been 'a little merry'.

But we still had business to attend to, and unfortunately, that business was a meeting with the local Magistrate to get the go-ahead to carry out inquiries, a necessity in a foreign country. Tim and I once more climbed into the police car and were driven across town, stopping briefly en route to pick up a very attractive interpreter who was to assist us in our meeting. Not long after, we pulled up outside the Magistrates' Office, and Tim turned to look at me. The pastis had hit, and I should imagine I was looking a little dishevelled: clothes perhaps a little crumpled, eyes a little unfocused. I think back now and imagine perhaps a little cartoon 'hic' escaping my lips, but perhaps I'm being unfair to myself. Whatever he saw led him to say, 'Yaki, I think you should stay in the car!'

I did as I was told. Tim headed off, enchanting interpreter in tow, while I closed my eyes in an attempt to sleep off the potent apéritif a little.

Tim later told me the magistrate was a very nice man who, through the interpreter, greeted him warmly and then proceeded to ask questions about our investigation. Being a bit of a cheeky so-and-so, after every exchange, Tim informed the interpreter he thought she was very attractive. In a professional manner, she ignored these remarks and carried on with her job.

At the end of the interview, Tim got up to leave, and the magistrate said, in perfect English, 'I hope you and Officer Brind have a pleasant stay in Lyon.' Tim suddenly realised he had understood everything that had been said throughout the meeting – including the extra exchanges with the interpreter. I chuckled when Tim told me this and informed him that it served him right!

Following this, Tim and the interpreter hopped back in the car. We dropped her back to her office and were then told by our host that we were heading for the favourite watering hole of Lyon's drug squad, a restaurant and bar in the centre of the city. I was feeling a little better by then but had a good idea of what was coming … and that meant 'Goodbye World!' A lovely meal was had by all that night, and the conversation, laughs, wine and stories flowed.

Over many years of meeting up with cops or ex-cops, I've come to realise that, in many ways, they're the same the World over – but not in all ways. That night in Lyon, we established that our host, a senior officer whose rank was the equivalent of a UK superintendent, had been in London two weeks earlier, 'Looking for a drug dealer called John'. That's literally what he told the Metropolitan Police, and I can only imagine what their response was. But that didn't deter him, and he spent a pleasant week in London, taken care of by the expenses account, looking for a needle in a haystack.

At the end of the night, we were driven back to the hotel we had been booked into, which we then discovered belonged to a mate of the chief. We later found out that – spoiler alert – this was no coincidence.

The next morning, we were picked up by the chief and his detective, both of whom could speak a little English. We sped through the beautiful French countryside and eventually turned off the main route to roll up at a vineyard, which was – surprise, surprise – owned by another mate of the chief.

We weren't complaining, however, and happily accepted the owner's invitation to tuck into the numerous 'samples'. After working our way through everything on offer, we headed back to the squad car only to see two cases of wine being loaded into the boot – and no money changing hands.

We set off back to the city along country roads. Suddenly, the chief slammed his hand on the dashboard and ordered his detective to stop. What on Earth was going on? He leapt out of the car and started clambering over a low fence. Tim and I looked at each other, confused. What had he seen? A wanted man, perhaps, or a crime in progress? Should we get out and lend a hand? We looked back only to see him reaching up to the heavily laden trees beyond the fence, and all became clear. He was 'scrumping': helping himself to some of the biggest, juiciest peaches I'd ever seen. Before long, he climbed back into the car with his haul, laughing. The detective turned back to Tim and me and said with a gleeful grin, 'He has wine in the boot and peaches along the dashboard!' We laughed along, of course, but inside, I was thinking, 'I know not all UK officers are totally straight up, but I can't imagine any of them doing what he's just done!' That night, we again ended up at the drug squad's favourite haunt, and once more, the food was good, and the alcohol was flowing. Happily for me, this time, it was Tim who was tipped over the edge.

The next day dawned. Some policing work took place, followed by a visit to the home of another detective, which involved more drink (no surprise there), and then we found ourselves en route to the home of the owner of that favourite Lyon bar-restaurant. We stopped to pick up the chief from the rather dowdy apartment block where he lived and expressed our surprise that a senior officer lived in such a place. 'Oh no,' grinned the detective. 'This is his city apartment. He has a 15-bedroom chateau in the countryside.' Everything started to make sense.

Arriving at the restaurant owner's house, we were shown to the rear of the property and a log cabin surrounded by a sunny veranda, upon which were three flower pots, each containing a plant with which Tim and I were very familiar. The spiked leaves, the pungent odour ... these were unmistakable. Cannabis.

Tim and I just looked at each other. As seasoned cops, we weren't shocked by the presence of the plants per se ... we were just very surprised to see them so openly on display in the present company! Laughing so as not to offend, I pointed out the obvious: 'You do know these are illegal in the UK?' To which the chief replied, 'Here too!' With a hearty Gallic chuckle, he then took out his handcuffs and laughingly arrested our hosts – after which we all posed for a photo. Another boozy evening ensued.

The next day, following an unexpected lunchtime visit to the city's gendarmerie training school Tim and I found ourselves seated – woefully under-dressed in our drug squad uniform of jumpers and jeans – at the top table in front of rows of smartly dressed young police officers, we were invited back to our detective driver's home for dinner.

The evening started, and the couple were great hosts. Of course, the drinks were flowing, the conversation was good, and before long, the food was ready. We didn't know what to expect when it came to French home cooking, but the first course was comfortingly familiar: cabbage and bacon. We tucked in.

Then the main course arrived, and Tim and I exchanged glances. There, carefully presented on each of our plates, was a whole quail, head and all. The poor little bird was looking up at me, and I tried to avoid its gaze. But I didn't want to insult our hosts, and nor did Tim, so we each pushed the head of the bird to one side before bravely soldiering on.

Quail conquered, the evening continued, and, again, it was a lovely one – and enlightening, too, when it came to the French police's approach to firearms. In my career, I've been lucky enough to talk to police officers from many different countries, and they are always astounded to discover that we don't bear arms in the UK. In fact, in the whole of my 32 years in service, I have never fired a gun.

Our host's response to this discovery was the same, and he preceded to tell us of the time when he had been out drinking and accidentally left his gun in a nightclub – and, even worse, of when he returned home one evening to find his two-year-old son standing at the top of the stairs with his gun in his hands! It was an education, and stories like his never fail to make me feel the approach to guns here in the UK is the right one.

The next day, we were headed home after an eye-opening week and some successful inquiries (yes, we did get some actual police work done!). Just as we were checking out of our hotel, the chief arrived and hit us with the final curve ball of the trip. As we stood there, he directed his mate, the owner of the hotel, to give us a bill for two weeks! It was confirmed as if we needed it: the chief was as bent as a nine-bob note. We were gobsmacked and had quite a job to convince him that this was not what UK cops are about and that we would pay only what we owed for the week: that was it. But that, as we found, was Lyon for you. It had been an education.

In 1983, I moved away from the Drugs Squad for a period. A new tenure policy had been introduced, which required us to move departments every few years in an attempt to ensure corruption – such as that of the disgraced Brighton Officers – was inhibited. As a result, I was placed with Hove CID ... but it was a move that didn't work out so well for my family life.

One day at work, I received a phone call from Ford Prison from an inmate on remand named Gary Scott, whom I'd arrested a short while previously. He told me the guy he was banged up with had confessed to the 'Body in the Boot' murder, a notorious case where a decomposing corpse had been found in a car at Gatwick Airport.

I contacted the Detective Superintendent in charge of the investigation, Doug Cheall, and shortly after, he and I visited Gary in prison to get a written statement. We met him in private, out of sight of other prisoners, and took the statement. The end of my involvement ... or so I thought.

A few months later, I was at work when I received a phone call from Thelma. Her voice was a little jittery as she told me she had answered our home phone to a call from Gary Scott, asking to talk to me. She said I was at work, so he asked her to relay a message: there was a contract out to kill him because he had spoken to us about the murder, so he had fled to Perth in Australia, and he wouldn't be attending court to give evidence.

I immediately contacted Doug, who visited Thelma to tell her Scott was an important witness and very much needed in court, and advised her what she should say if he were to phone again. Thelma was not pleased about any of this, and I felt bad for her, too; she was and still is made of strong stuff, but she shouldn't have had to be involved in such things.

Not long after, Gary phoned my home for a second time, again when I was at work. This time, he said he was in Portugal. Thelma followed Doug's instructions but had no idea if Gary would be returning home, though the trial was about to start.

Little did we know that Gary was indeed on his way back to the UK – and he had found out where we lived.

GET YOUR COAT, YOU'RE NICKED!

The next call Thelma received from Gary frightened her – and for good reason. It was getting late in the evening; the kids were in bed, and as before, I wasn't there. The phone rang, and it was Gary: he was in Hove and was coming to see me. Thelma told him there was no point coming to the house, but he wasn't having any of it. Thelma must have been scared, but she acted quickly and sensibly: she ran upstairs to get the kids out of bed, intending to drive away before he got there ... but before she could leave, there was a knock at the front door.

Luckily, at that exact time, I pulled up outside the house. There, stood on my doorstep, was Gary Scott. Now, as with most informants, Gary Scott was not the most subtle of individuals. He had the words 'Cut here' tattooed around his neck, and, bearing in mind this was November, he was wearing a big cream hat and sunglasses because he was convinced he was being followed.

Despite my annoyance at what he had put Thelma and the kids through, I did actually ask him in. The guy seemed genuinely scared of his situation, but there was not a lot I could do at 10pm from my own house. Plying him with a Scotch or two, I managed to convince Gary to go home, which he eventually did, clutching the remainder of the whisky bottle. There was a huge sigh of relief from Thelma, and I was sure that was our last dealing with Gary Scott.

Six months later I received another phone call, this time at work, from Gary. He told me he knew of a criminal team that was producing counterfeit audio tapes of the UK Top 20. Again, his information turned out to be useful and resulted in the conviction of a quite unlikely bunch of middle-aged ladies who had been producing their fake goods from a very normal-looking terraced house, all of whom received surprisingly stiff sentences. This was indeed the last I heard of Gary Scott: he received a very generous £1000 for his information (when I had told him to expect £200) and skipped off happily into the sunset.

That wasn't the last of the counterfeit tapes, however. Detectives at that time, believe it or not, were allowed a 'Beer Allowance' – an incentive to hang around the sort of bars and clubs where information about criminal activity might be passed around. One such establishment was The Temple Bar, on the Brighton and Hove border in Western Road.

One day I was in the upstairs bar watching a guy called Steve Foster, the Captain of Brighton & Hove Albion, playing pool against Jack Broderick, who owned the whole place. They were halfway through a frame when Steve looked up and said to Jack, 'I've just remembered. I paid you for those tapes, and you said you'd get them to me today.'

Jack, realising I was sitting watching them, replied, 'Yeah, I know Steve. I'll get them for you later.'

Steve didn't get the hint. 'I know what you're like,' he said. 'I want to see what I've bought!'

With that, Jack put down his cue, went out to a back room, and came out with a plastic carrier bag.

Steve, who clearly still hadn't twigged, then said, 'Yeah, I know what you're like!' and tipped the entire bag of tapes onto the pool table. He proceeded to count them out to ensure he hadn't been diddled by Jack. Suddenly, Steve stopped. The 'On' switch had finally flicked in his head, and he realised he was counting counterfeit tapes on a pool table in front of a Police Detective.

Watching him flounder and dig was, I must admit, quite amusing. He turned to the guy who acted as his driver: 'Sledge, I've got your tapes here.' Poor Sledge didn't know what to do but eventually plumped to start shovelling the tapes back in the bag.

I decided that was the moment for me to speak up, though I was rather enjoying their discomfort: 'I had the team that made them arrested and charged a couple of weeks ago,' I laughed. But I left it there. I didn't have the heart to put them through any more.

I became involved in another international drug case in the spring of 1984, triggered by a tip that came through on an otherwise quiet Sunday morning, a time which, in the Drug Squad, was normally taken up with paperwork and cleaning the vehicles. Late morning we took a call from a DC I knew, Dick Duffield from Worthing CID, who told us he'd had a tip-off that we could expect to find two Peruvian men with a kilo of cocaine at a hotel in Worthing that afternoon. It sounded unlikely, but Dick was a good Detective, and we felt if he believed it, so should we.

My colleague Dave Tingle and I obtained a warrant, went to the hotel, and found two young Peruvian men in their early 20s who didn't put up a struggle. On searching the room, we found a holdall containing a package of a white substance, which turned out to be cocaine-based, under the beds, and this seizure turned out to be one of the largest by a Provincial Force ever. Happy days, for us cops, at least.

In the days and weeks that followed, it turned out there was more to the case than initially met the eye. First of all, it appeared that the white substance had already changed hands a few times within Worthing. The Peruvians had been trying to sell it to the local villains, who thought the two foreigners were out of their depth, so they had tied the Peruvians up and robbed them. However, they soon discovered that what they had was not the powder they expected; it was cocaine paste, which needs to undergo a process before it can be sold on the street and snorted ... so they gave it back and then informed them, hence our tip-off.

However, it also seemed Worthing's villains found out something that we focussed on once we got the Peruvians in for interview: the cocaine belonged to the South American Mafia.

Both men continued to be perfect prisoners, and once they got into the interview room, they didn't stop talking. They told the interviewers they were indeed part of a Mafia cocaine empire in Peru and involved in the export of thousands of kilos of the stuff. They had been in Milan and then Rome overseeing the cocaine production process when they caught wind of an imminent police raid and fled, grabbing the bag of paste as they did so. They had a bit of money but not enough for flights back to Peru. Their intention was to sell the cocaine to fund their return home, and they made their way to Worthing (which one of them was familiar with) to do so.

GET YOUR COAT, YOU'RE NICKED!

The information kept flowing from these two men, including lots about how they operated their drug empire, which was really useful for many other Drug Agencies, including the Drug Enforcement Administration. They talked so freely that we were granted extra time to interview them and established a dedicated space from which to coordinate everything – albeit the Force Incident Caravan parked in the car park of Worthing nick. We passed information to the Peruvian law enforcement agencies, and this was sent in diplomatic bags to the UK Embassy in Peru.

The two men were eventually convicted at Lewes Crown Court, but because of their cooperation, they received relatively light sentences. In his summing up, the judge complimented Sussex Police for their work, which was gratifying for all involved. But the most satisfying thing about the whole case was knowing that thanks to a tip-off relayed to us one quiet Sunday morning, we had nabbed two men in the UK with a kilo of cocaine, and the information gathered had led to the arrest of nine people in Rotterdam plus 25 kilos of cocaine seized in Italy and 150 kilos of cocaine seized in Peru. We also later found out that a corrupt Peruvian police officer was moved from Drugs Investigations to Traffic Enforcement. All in all, that's what I call a result.

In the autumn of that year, something happened on my patch that made headlines around the World: the Brighton Bombing. In the early hours of 12 October 1984, the IRA set off a bomb in the Grand Hotel on Brighton's seafront during the Conservative Party conference. Five people were killed and 31 were injured, though the then-Prime Minister Margaret Thatcher narrowly escaped the explosion. I heard the shocking news that morning when I got up to get ready for my 8 a.m. to 4 p.m. shift and switched on the TV to see the footage of fire, smoke and flashing blue lights as the injured were stretchered out from the debris. When I arrived at work, it was quite literally Action Stations, and the frenzy of activity continued for months. I wasn't involved in the investigation, as when I first arrived at Brighton, I ended up snowed under by other cases and had to pick up the slack from those who were involved in it. It was at least a year before things got back to normal at Brighton nick.

The following year, poor Thelma again got pulled into a situation she shouldn't have had to worry about. I had been investigating a case of what we used to call 'bilking' – a lodger who had done a runner without paying his rent. The guy who owed money was a Libyan national and well-known in the Hove area, as he played football at quite a good standard. I found out where he was living and arrested him. On examination of his passport, I found that he was an overstayer which meant we needed to contact the immigration services. He was charged, then rearrested by immigration and taken into custody to await deportation. All this happened not long after police officer Yvonne Fletcher had been murdered, shot from inside the Libyan Embassy in London, and also in the wake of the deaths of several exiled opponents of Gadaffi's regime in Manchester and London. I went home that night and again found Thelma shaken; someone had phoned our home and, when Thelma answered, told her he knew where we lived and which school our young children attended and that there would be consequences unless our Libyan prisoner was released. On that occasion, we did nothing; the Libyan overstayer was deported, and nothing further was heard.

It would be impossible to overstate the gratitude I feel for Thelma's unending love and support over the years.

She's gone through so much being a detective's wife (or I should say my wife), and I don't know of any other who's had to put up with everything she's endured. Quite apart from the potential threat from the Libyans and Gary Scotts of this world, she's had to put up with rarely knowing where I am or what I'm up to; in fact, she once received an anonymous call from someone (who I'd probably once nicked) who asked, 'Where do you think your husband is?'

'Working,' She had replied.

'No,' he said. 'He's out with his blonde girlfriend.' I was, in fact, working with Sally Luck, a very good Drug Squad colleague with whom I was partnered at the time. Thelma didn't bat an eyelid, put the phone down and got on with her day.

During my long and unpredictable working hours, she was always there, bringing up our wonderful children and making sure I had a home and loving family to (eventually) return home to. She supported every decision I made, including not going up through the ranks; I'm sure she would have enjoyed the nice dresses and fancy cruises the higher pay would have brought, as well as the kudos and invitations to the Superintendent's dance and what have you – but she always supported me in that decision. I couldn't have done it without her, and for that and a million other things, I will be forever grateful.

One part of the job that some Officer's wives didn't like was the need for us to frequent the sort of bars, pubs and clubs where we might pick up valuable information. One we spent a fair bit of time in was The Temple Bar … and unsurprisingly, a number of colourful events occurred on these premises.

One evening, Tony Bell, my partner in Hove CID, and I were in The Temple Bar when a man walked in and started to speak to Jack, the bar's owner. We were then introduced to 'Doctor George,' as he was known. Apparently, he had started to frequent The Temple Bar, which I immediately thought was strange, a man of his position frequenting a 'villain's boozer,' so I was interested in getting him chatting.

A black guy in his mid-30s, he said he was working as a doctor at the Royal Sussex County Hospital in Kemp Town, Brighton. He came across as pretty knowledgeable, but for me, alarm bells were ringing. Having been on the Drug Squad for many years, I had picked up bits of medical information and just knew something wasn't right.

The next few times Tony and I were in the bar, George was there, and we would have a few drinks with him. Each time we met, my suspicions grew until one time he told me his full name, which was very unusual, 'George Zic Woppi Opio'. As soon as I could, I made enquiries at the Royal Sussex which had never heard of him, and nor was he on the GMC Doctors list. I made further enquiries and found he had been on a

Pharmaceutical degree course at Brighton University but had dropped out after a year.

About a week later, we were in the bar when one of Jack's regulars said the day before, he had been walking past the Clock Tower in the centre of Brighton and saw George in his car. He said he'd just been involved in an accident, and the guy helped him push the car to one side of the road. With George already in my sights, I made more enquiries and found he'd made a claim on his car insurance for this accident … but also, he had no driving licence, meaning the claim would be fraudulent.

The plot was thickening. George was clearly a very slippery character – so again, I delved further. I discovered he was working as a bookkeeper for a company in Shoreham, so the next morning, Tony Bell and I headed over there. When we entered his office, George just looked up at us and said, 'Oh, hello, Yaki and Tony. What are you doing here?'

I just replied, 'Get your coat, George. You're nicked!'

Flustered, all he could say was: 'What have I done?'

Back at the station, I informed him of him the reasons for his arrest, delivered the official caution and told him we, as police officers, didn't like being lied to. He admitted the offences, was charged and bailed and was never again seen in The Temple Bar. I hoped we'd seen the back of him and his lies for good.

On a Sunday morning about two months later, I was doing paperwork in the CID Office when a female Special Constable came quietly into the office. She was very subdued, though she clearly had something to say.

I asked if I could help her, and she said, 'I think I need to speak to someone.' We went into an unoccupied room, where she proceeded to tell me a very sad story that angered me intensely.

Being quite young, she still lived with her mum and stepdad, and when she'd recently found herself with a cough and sore throat she just couldn't get rid of, her stepdad had told her he had a friend called George who was a doctor, and he could treat her.

At the mention of his name, my heckles were raised. I feared what was coming. She went on to tell me Doctor George had checked her chest and throat and then given her an internal examination. The poor girl. I felt so sorry for her and was determined this man would not get away with it.

I asked Tony to come with me to once again nick our old mate George. We arrived at his house at about 1 p.m. just as his wife was dishing out Sunday dinner for them, their children and her parents. I slapped on the handcuffs and stuck him in the back of the car.

Back at Hove Police Station he was charged but frustratingly, and despite my pleas, then bailed and told to report to the Magistrates Court. George walked out through the doors onto the streets … and was never seen again. His name has been etched in my brain ever since, but the worst thing is we let down our Special Constable.

Another Sunday morning (what was it about Sundays?), at around the same time I was at home when Jack, owner of The Temple Bar, phoned to tell me there had been an incident at the bar the night before. That wasn't unusual in itself, but what was unexpected was that this had involved two Brighton Detectives, and he wanted to find out what the upshot had been.

Apparently, they'd come into the bar a bit worse for wear and not behaving like Officers should. They were being a bit arrogant, had insulted the girlfriends of two of his regular customers, and a punch-up had ensued, resulting in a 999 call and their detention.

I contacted Brighton nick and was told the Detectives had been well out of order, and it was unlikely that, despite them being good Officers and the incident being out of character, they would keep their jobs. The next day, I popped in to see Jack, who gave me the blow-by-blow account of what the detectives had done, and there was no doubt they had been out of order. I told him they would be losing their jobs over but Jack was astounded.

'Oh no, they don't deserve that,' he said. 'I just thought they'd get a bollocking.' He went on to say he'd seen far worse antics in his career: 'They were just trying to show off,' he said.

He asked what he should do; he didn't want them to lose their careers. I told him the only option was to go to Brighton Police Station, speak to the officer dealing with the matter and change his statement, but it had nothing to do with me. I was annoyed at what the two Detectives had done, but ultimately, it was Jack's decision. He went to the station, changed his statement, and the two lucky Detectives kept their careers, eventually retiring after 30 years in the force. They never knew it was me who influenced my mate Jack and allowed them to avoid leaving the service in disgrace.

In 1987, I returned to the Drugs Squad in Hove as Drugs Intelligence West. This was an office (or rather, hut behind the Police Station) role that involved organizing intelligence on a dated Trivector Triton computer and undeniably signalled a stepping back from the hands-on action and occasional danger of the roles I had held previously. However, by now, I was nearly 40 years old and had been on the Force for 23 years; I didn't mind a little less excitement.

My next career move came in 1991 when I took on the job of Sussex Police Chemist Inspector, a unique role with a lot of responsibility. I was tasked with visiting pharmacies and other dispensing drug agencies to examine their records and was largely left to my own devices. As a police officer, I could not be refused access during working hours, although a number of dispensing doctors surgeries did try.

It wasn't unusual for me to find that, once I established discrepancies in pharmacy records, it was because the pharmacist or doctor in charge was helping themselves. One such case involved a female doctor who was making out prescriptions to patients for Valium but taking them herself. She was incredibly distraught when I confronted her with what I had found out, but she temporarily removed herself from the British Medical Association and got treatment for her addiction. In that case, I felt I had helped an otherwise respectable profession to realise she needed help.

GET YOUR COAT, YOU'RE NICKED!

Less satisfying was the case shortly after that involved a pharmacy in Lancing. While going through the Controlled Drug Register, I noticed that there was an unusually large number of prescriptions for a drug called Diconal, a heroin-based tablet. I queried this with the pharmacist, who told me he also thought it a bit strange as the Doctor prescribing it, who worked in the psychiatric ward at the local hospital, had said he was visiting these patients himself and would deliver them personally.

Alarm bells immediately sounded, so I took the details of the patients' names on the prescriptions and paid each a visit. None had even heard of the drug, let alone taken it. Armed with my statements, I went to the hospital, found the doctor in his department and arrested him for unlawful possession of a controlled drug and criminal deception. He was then escorted out of the hospital and taken home so we could search for his stash of drugs.

Sadly, when we reached his home, where he lived with his wife and three-year-old son, we didn't have to look far. On the coffee table in the lounge, right by where his son was playing, was a syringe and needle with the residue of a pink substance in it. He clearly had a very bad drug problem.

The doctor was then taken to Shoreham Police Station to be interviewed, and we discovered he had only recently started at Southland Hospital. He had moved there from another hospital, and when we made enquiries there, it transpired that they quite possibly had suspected he had a drug problem and, rather than get him help and/or report him, they had simply ensured he got 'moved on' elsewhere.

What's more, anything I did discover from both hospitals was achieved without any help from the management; as I often found, at the first whiff of scandal, those high up in the hospital hierarchy would refuse to divulge any further information to me and I had to use 'detective means' to establish his history further.

What I found was that neither hospital had carried out checks on the information listed on his CV – and if they had, they would have found out he wasn't registered at the BMA and, therefore, was not allowed to practice. Eventually, the doctor pleaded guilty at Crown Court, and I believe he was given a prison sentence that was suspended. At least he was no longer practising and, hopefully, as a family man, was getting help with his addiction.

As a part of my job, I was required to pay visits to all the pharmacies on my patch, and one sticks in my mind not because I found anything horrendous going on there – but because it seemed to have stayed stuck in the 1940s. As soon as I entered, I could see nothing in it had changed for about 50 years. The front counter had a glass sliding door, which was shattered and dangerous, and there was a bottle of cleaning product within reach of customers bearing the skull and crossbones symbol, which indicates poison.

I asked to see the pharmacist and, after a wait out, shuffled an elderly gentleman well into his 80s. I asked to see his controlled drug cupboard, which by law had to be a locked steel cabinet fixed to a wall or similar. He said he hadn't got one of those and kept those sorts of drugs in his chest of drawers in the back, which I found had no lock or key.

GET YOUR COAT, YOU'RE NICKED!

The pharmacist was a lovely guy, but it appeared all the laws made in the previous 50 years had passed him by. It was fairly obvious to me that he just loved talking to the public and dispensing what few prescriptions he was given.

I didn't want to throw the book at him, but clearly, I couldn't allow him to continue as he was. I stepped out for a while to think and decided to try to persuade the pharmacist to close up and retire. Thankfully, his son had arrived, and he helped me persuade his dad to call time on the operation. He closed the shop for good that day, which was sad, but it had to be done.

I was pretty independent when it came to decision-making during my time as Police Chemist Inspector but did occasionally run into opposition – and on one occasion, I came into serious conflict with the Detective Chief Inspector.

My job included notifying the Home Office of all addicts who were collecting their drugs from the county's dispensaries. I had to collate all their details, which, of course, was privileged and confidential information, and submit them to the Home Office Drugs Branch. One afternoon, DCI John Byford came into my office to say he wanted all the details I held of the addicts in the area as he wanted to pass them on to another agency.

I told him no; I wouldn't do it as it would be a breach of the Data Protection Act. To say he was not happy with my reply was an understatement: in fact, as soon as I said it, I saw the connecting door between my office and the Sergeant's office (who I came under) slowly close as, he said afterwards, he 'Didn't want to witness what might come next!' The DCI and

I had words. I stood my ground, and he eventually left, saying, 'If you don't do it, I'll find somebody that will.'

The next day, I contacted the Police Federation Office for advice and was told that what the DCI had instructed me to do was indeed unlawful – but in our disciplined profession, I had to obey an order. However, if he continued to insist, he would have to put the order in writing.

Some days later, John Byford returned to the office and asked how far I had gotten with his request. He was not a happy bunny when I told him of the Federation's advice. He made a hasty exit, and I never heard or saw him again in our office. I was just glad I was able to resolve the issue with my integrity intact.

It was during my time as Police Chemist Inspector that something happened that continues to have a great bearing on me today. It happened outside of work, but it bears telling here because, in some ways, I feel it puts my working life into perspective.

Throughout the '80s and '90s, Thelma and I had been able to enjoy more foreign travel together, and in 1994, we treated ourselves to a trip to Antalya in Turkey. We'd been there a few days when we decided a day on the beach was in order and were both enjoying soaking up the sun and, for once, having nothing to do.

Suddenly, out of the corner of my eye, I saw something wasn't right with Thelma, and I sat up – only to see she had collapsed. I rushed to her, and to my horror, she was totally limp and expressionless, with her eyes rolled back in her head.

I grasped her shoulders and shook her, calling her name in an attempt to rouse her – but got no response. She was showing no signs of life.

Desperate, I started screaming for help – though to whom I had no idea. I knew no one, and the only people in the vicinity were holidaymakers of who-knows-what nationality in their bathing costumes. I felt for her pulse, and try as might, I could find nothing.

To my eternal gratitude, at that moment, two Dutch women, who turned out to be nurses, came running to Thelma's aid. They had a bottle of water and started splashing her in the face, but she didn't respond. Even to this day, though I have replayed the scene a thousand times in my head, I struggle to explain how I felt in those seconds and minutes. All I can say is I had seen many dead bodies in my career, and at that time, I could see, I was sure, she had died. I was looking at my wife, my everything, dead on a beach in the middle of nowhere.

Then, suddenly, what seemed like a miracle occurred. Thelma let out a low groan; she moved her head slightly, and her eyelids started to flicker. She was alive. I think I probably cried in relief.

A few hours later, Thelma had recovered and we were talking about the event. She asked me why someone crossed her arms over her chest (that didn't happen) and told me that while she had been out of it, she had had a wonderful dream where she met her deceased Nanny and Grandad. She had experienced some sort of near-death experience.

Frighteningly, a few years later, a similar incident occurred, again on holiday and this time when we were on a paddle steamer going down the Mississippi River. She came out of the shower in our cabin and collapsed on the bed, her eyes wide open. Again, I was terrified: there was no doctor on board and only 400 passengers. Happily, she came around, but we ended up having to dock the ship and take a trip to a local hospital so she could get checked out. Thankfully, she was OK, and perhaps the incident was a little less shocking this second time.

However, both incidents, and the one in Turkey in particular, have deeply affected me from that day to this. As a police officer, I became used to dealing with stressful and frightening situations. I've seen some pretty horrible things over the years, which is not surprising considering the areas of policing I've worked in. There was the 22-year-old guy, his whole life in front of him, dead on a ratty sofa, having drowned in his own vomit. I've met countless addicts, wasting their lives in pursuit of the next fix; petty (and not so petty) criminals, inflicting misery on their victims; and some of the saddest cases, the sex workers on the streets of Brighton, often young people who had turned to what they were doing out of desperation. But in the main, I never took any of it home. I left my work at work, always returning to my home and family as an escape from what I encountered on the streets.

The one exception to this is the road traffic accident I encountered in December 1964. I admit I have never forgotten the girl I cradled in my lap and who later died. In the weeks and months after, I tried hard to forget I was the last person to talk to her and to cope with the feeling I may have made the wrong decision in not getting her into the ambulance first. To this day, I can picture her face, and the memory still brings me to tears.

Nowadays, police officers are encouraged to speak up if they are having trouble coping with something they have encountered at work and offered help; there was none of that available in my day. Even if I had opened up to someone at the time, there was no support. We were just expected to get on with it.

But apart from that girl, nothing at work ever affected me in the way I felt when I believed I might have lost Thelma; she herself will say, although I've never cried in front of her or the kids after that incident in Turkey, I've been a different guy. She says I'm more emotional in a way I never was before. I may have been, in the words of the Duty Seargent at Sandgate, a 'rufty, tufty policeman', but one thing will always terrify me and leave me feeling powerless and in tears: the thought of being without my wonderful wife.

In 1996, at a time when retirement was looming over my shoulder, I met my old colleague Dick Dufield at a leaving do. Knowing I soon had some big life decisions to make, I found what he had to say very interesting: he was working for American Express alongside another ex-colleague, Ken Becks, and his own position at the Brighton office was about to become vacant as he was moving abroad. I filed the conversation away in my mind under 'Very Interesting'.

In October of that year, my own retirement party took place in the bar at Shoreham Police Station, where I had started my career (in the station, not the bar) some 32 years earlier. Being Police Chemist Inspector, I had made the invites out to look like prescriptions, and the turnout was more than I could have hoped for. Of course, all my mates were there, including Bob Batey, who had been there at the beginning, but even the Assistant Chief Constable John Abbott, who I had played football and worked with in the early 1970s in Brighton when he was a PC, made an effort to come along for a few beers.

It has always been the tradition in the Drug Squad to give out silly presents when leaving, and as the longest-ever serving Drug Squad Officer in the country, I thought I should go the extra mile: Tony Baker was presented with a tankard inscribed 'The Best Drug Detective'; Glenn Smith from Hove CID got one inscribed 'The Best Crime Detective'; and Tim Carter and Malcolm 'Streaky' Bacon received framed photos of our trips abroad. In return, I was presented with two etched paintings, one of 'The Cross' at Chichester, which was one of my first stations, and one of The Royal Pavilion in Brighton, where I spent many years.

Despite having a great leaving do, it was a sad day when I left. I'd known nothing else since leaving school. In the run-up to it, I'd even tried to argue I should be allowed to stay on as a civilian Chemist Inspector but was told there was no funding for it. At the time, I wasn't too happy – but what came next led me to be very grateful for the decision. 'Retirement' really worked out for me: my career wasn't over, not by a long shot. And neither were the adventures.

The French Detective (left), Yaki and Tim Carter.

Tim Carter, with the Senior Officer from Lyon, putting handcuffs on the host, cannabis plant in the foreground.

LISBON   JULY 1982

OVERSEA   ENQUIRY ON OPERATION ZURICH

WITH   STREAKY BACON

Yaki in Lisbon on a cocaine investigation.

CHAPTER 6: FORGET THE PIPE AND SLIPPERS

I may have been officially retired from the police – but I wasn't yet ready for the armchair, pipe and slippers. I contacted Ken Betts and, after a very informal interview with Kevin Gallagher, a retired senior police officer from New York who was by then Vice President of Amex's Global Security in Europe, the Middle East, Africa and the Far East, I was offered a job as Special Agent for American Express. This meant I would be providing evidence to law enforcement agencies around the world to help them track down and prosecute anyone trying to commit fraud against the company.

There was time for a little relaxation first, however. Before taking up my position, Thelma and I took an amazing month-long holiday in the Far East, something I had always promised I would do when I retired. We had a wonderful time in Singapore, Bali, Hong Kong, Bangkok and Phuket before setting off back home to the next phase of our lives.

In January 1997, I took my place in the Amex office alongside Ken and Hazel Cooper, who also had a policing connection in that I knew her husband as he was a Brighton police officer. From the start, my new colleagues and I got on very well, and I was very glad I had managed to find such a great place to launch the second phase of my working life.

GET YOUR COAT, YOU'RE NICKED!

Not long after I joined Amex, Kevin Gallagher said to me, 'Yak, this is how I look at it: we used to have a 'proper' job once, now this is a bolt-on career,' and he was right. The salary was very generous, half as good again as I had been getting as a Senior Detective, and I had a flash ID card which showed I was a Special Agent. The expenses package was also incredible: I was given an American Express Corporate Card to pay for taking Officers out for food and drinks with the words, 'Whatever the Police want, they get.' This was intended as a thank you for supporting Amex in their investigations, and Amex was good to its word on this: in the entire time I worked for the company, my expenses were never queried, though it wasn't uncommon for them to reach four figures.

One of the first notable cases I worked on at Amex involved a guy called Gino Hunter. I had received information that an American Express card had been hit up for over £11,000, and the evidence was pointing to Gino, whose name I recognised because he had been arrested for robbery by Hove CID when I worked there – though his Amex application stated he was a double glazing salesman.

Unfortunately, he hadn't paid back the money. I prepared the evidential bundle and personally took the file over to my old office in Hove, where I spoke to a Detective Sergeant who said he would allocate it to a Detective Constable. About six weeks later, I received a phone call from a DC who said she had contacted the owner of the double glazing company whose number had been supplied on Gino's application form, and he had confirmed all the details on it were correct.

Smelling a very obvious rat, I delved further. 'Where did you get the number?' She confirmed it was from the Amex application form, which had been submitted by Gino Hunter. She informed me no crime had been committed, so this must be considered a civil debt, and therefore, there would be no further Police involvement in the case.

I wasn't having that. I told her about Hunter's arrest some years earlier and explained how that meant the card application was indeed fraudulent. With that, the DC put the phone down on me.

As it turned out, two months later, Hunter was arrested and charged with criminal deception, to which he pleaded guilty, and he was later sentenced to 18 months imprisonment. However, my disappointment at the attitude of that DC and at how my old CID office had dealt with the whole matter marked the start of my disillusionment with the police service.

Another case from my early days at Amex was that of Aussie Rick. I answered my desk phone to a man who introduced himself as 'Aussie Rick'. The guy claimed he knew of an Amex employee who had disclosed private details about a cardholder, and this had resulted in fraud on the account. This was interesting information, so after a bit of to-ing and fro-ing, we arranged to meet.

Six weeks later, we met in a hotel in Bournemouth. The guy was a strange character but pleasant enough. He gave me a bit more information about the fraud, which seemed plausible, and then the conversation turned to what he wanted for this information: £30,000. In my 30+ years in policing, the most money I had ever been able to get for an informant was £200 for Gary Scott! I knocked Aussie Rick down to £20,000 but told him I'd need to get higher approval.

The next morning, I contacted Kevin Gallagher and told him all about it. He thought about it for about 20 seconds and said, 'We'll pay it!' I was unsettled, to say the least: we were going to pay an untried informant £20,000 on my say-so, albeit in small increments, so we could steadily access more information and work out who was responsible for the fraud.

The next step was to get the first bit of cash. With Kevin's authority for £3,000 cash in my hand, I paid a visit to Amex's own in-house bank and further requested they give it to me in a plain brown envelope. The cashier gave me a curious look and said she needed to seek authority from her supervisor, but when they realised which department I had come from, I was handed the bulging package.

Again, I met up with Aussie Rick, this time in the glamorous surroundings of a Little Chef 30 miles on my side of Bournemouth. He was able to give me more details of accounts he believed either had or were being compromised, and in exchange, I passed the envelope to him under the table.

On checking these accounts, we discovered all had been compromised, and all were fairly new, and from there, it didn't take long for to establish how the fraud was occurring. At that time, the task of checking new applications was outsourced to a company in the West Midlands. As each application was approved, Amex was notified, and a card was sent out to the applicant's address.

We were able to identify one employee who had dealt with all the compromised accounts. It appeared he was taking down applicants' details and passing them on to a mate who then made contact with American Express, stating he had just moved from the address on the application. Thanks to the information passed on to him by the crooked employee, he was able to pass all security questions put to him by Amex, and so a new address was registered, and the card was sent there, directly into the hands of the fraudsters. As soon as the card arrived, it was used and then abandoned.

Now we knew how the fraud was being committed, we needed to gather some concrete evidence – and for that, we needed the input of the West Midlands police and to register Aussie Rick with them as an informant. Kevin and I travelled to Birmingham and put things in place, which meant the police were now the lead on this investigation; what's more, it was now vital that everything was done by the book if we were going to provide convincing evidence in court.

The main thing we needed to prove was that this particular employee was at his computer terminal when the activity took place and that he was taking notes of what he saw on the screen. To do this, the police had to clone the computer and place a camera in position, so they sought and secured the agreement of the company to help them do this. Things seemed to be going well until we got some frustrating news: despite agreeing to the plan that would secure the evidence we needed, the company had moved our suspect from Amex

Applications to another department. We were not best pleased – but at least the fraudulent activity had been stopped. Aussie Rick wasn't happy either when I told him he wouldn't be getting any more money – and as far as I was concerned, that was the last I would be seeing of him.

Two weeks later, I received a phone call from the Custody Sergeant at Bournemouth Police Station. He said he had a man in custody on a charge of domestic violence who wanted me to know he had been arrested. It was Aussie Rick. Of course, that wasn't his real name, but they knew what it was, thanks to the fact they had found his passport.

I had already thought there must be something more to this guy than he was letting on, and this prompted me to do some digging. I phoned the Australian Embassy and managed to get hold of an Australian Police Officer who was very helpful and who was able to uncover some very interesting information: the guy I knew as Aussie Rick was wanted by the Greater Manchester Police for a fraud committed six years previously under his real name.

Later that day, the plot further thickened. The 'Fraudster Previously Known As Aussie Rick' phoned me to say he was out of custody and on his way to Brighton, and if I got him a hotel for the night, he could give me information about another job, this time in London. Though it sounded promising, I had to be very careful. I was now dealing with a wanted man who was also registered as an informant with West Midlands Police under a fake name.

This time, we met at a small hotel on Brighton's seafront, and I checked him in using my Amex Card. He started to tell me what he knew about a team of South London fraudsters, but I had to tell him I needed to contact the Metropolitan Police to transfer his informant details to them.

I returned to the office to speak to the Detectives in Greater Manchester who had dealt with the case from six years previously. I explained what had happened and that we had to work out a plan as I didn't want my informant thinking I had 'bubbled him up' and the Officer told me what had happened in the case: Aussie Rick had proposed to his girlfriend but told her he had no money and borrowed over £6,000 from her to buy an engagement ring. He then ran off with the ring. The case had even made the front page of The Sun newspaper.

With Rick still none the wiser, I arranged for him to meet up with two Metropolitan Police Detectives in a coffee bar in South London – and thought this time I'd heard the last of him. Not a chance. That afternoon, I got a phone call from none other than Aussie Rick. He said he was sitting in the back of a police car, having been arrested for a fraud he'd committed in Manchester.

I feigned huge shock at what he had told me but was also genuinely surprised he was phoning me whilst on his way to the cells. Thankfully, all then went quiet on the Aussie Rick front, and I later heard he had received a sentence of two years imprisonment.

End of the story? Sadly not! Two years later, he was released, and who was the first person he called? Me.

I couldn't believe I was hearing from him again, but at least our chat was brief. He told me he was going back to Australia and wanted the rest of his money from the original Amex fraud that had first brought us into contact. I told him it wasn't possible, made my excuses and hung up. However, the next day, I told Kevin about our conversation and we decided, with a view to finally getting rid of him, we should offer him £250 and have done with it. He happily accepted, and I actually took the step of flying up to Manchester to meet him at the airport so I could put the money in his hand and say goodbye. As I did so, I thought: 'This is the end now. No more Aussie Rick.'

But, like all good horror movies … Six weeks later, my phone rang, and down the line, I heard an unmistakable voice. It was Aussie Rick. Though thankfully, now in Australia.

'Yaki, you've had an armed robbery at your Amex Office in Melbourne. They've nicked all the currency and buried it in a garden, and I know where.'

I told him I'd check it out and call him back. I phoned my sister office in Sydney, and they confirmed the story was true. But they also said their equivalent of our National Crime Squad was all over it. This gave me a bit of a problem: I certainly didn't want to tell Aussie Rick this in case he forewarned the culprits. So I fobbed him off by saying I was having trouble getting hold of my counterparts in Australia and I'd phone him back tomorrow – which I never did. And that really, truly was the last I ever heard of Aussie Rick … though there's always tomorrow.

GET YOUR COAT, YOU'RE NICKED!

In 2002, I picked up another job, which seemed strange from the start. It appeared American Express accounts were being opened in Virginia, USA, but being used in Scotland of all places and then ditched. The transactions didn't involve large amounts of money on each card – perhaps three or four thousand pounds, but there were many cards involved.

We had no suspects or arrests, so I had to get a police officer interested, which was not going to be easy. I eventually spoke to a Detective Constable in the Lothian and Borders Financial Crime Unit in Edinburgh, who said he would look into it, so I passed him all the information I had, which included names and addresses as well as account numbers. I then got in touch with the police in Virginia – and their reaction was entirely different: as far as they were concerned this was a fraud involving US dollars, and so needed to be taken very seriously indeed.

The case went on for months, and of course I kept abreast of it but wasn't expecting what happened next: I was invited to a meeting to discuss the case at the US Secret Service HQ in Washington DC. I was a little taken aback and also a little flattered and intrigued; a one to one with a Secret Service Agent sounded like a very interesting experience, so I accepted the invitation.

I booked my flights and a nice hotel room (thanks, Amex!) and, a few weeks later, touched down in Washington. I arrived at the conference centre where the meeting was to be held and was ushered to a large conference room where I found over 70 Officers gathered to talk about the case. I don't know what I expected, but it wasn't anything on that scale!

Unbeknown to me, this fraud was of high interest to the Secret Service as, apparently, its remit is to protect all US Senior Politicians and the American financial state, and this American Express fraud came under that.

There was more: I was told that, as the only UK representative, I was on the panel and directed to sit at the top table. As proceedings continued I was then asked to stand up and present the UK side of events. Despite this rather daunting audience, which included Arnold Schwarzenegger lookalikes of the type I'd seen guarding US Presidents, I'm glad to say all went smoothly, and no one asked any awkward questions. What's more, I came home with a mug bearing the Virginia police logo, which, like everything in the States, is bigger and better than any I've ever seen.

A couple of years later, having been at Amex for nearly seven years, I was promoted to Senior Special Agent. This came with quite a good uplift to my salary and a yearly bonus, which I split with Hazel in the office.

That same year, American Express Global Security had their Special Agents World Meeting at the Bellagio Hotel in Las Vegas, USA. What an experience that was! We were flown Business Class to Las Vegas, and our hotel rooms were on the 24th floor of a very nice hotel. On the 26th floor was an Amex Security Suite, but for the duration of the conference, this became our own private bar where all drinks were free. Everything was paid for, and on the last night, we ate in the Fountain Restaurant, which had been reserved exclusively for us. Anything on their menu was ours to enjoy, including top-shelf drinks. Most of us working in Global Security from around the world were retired cops who work hard and play hard – and it was a great week. What's more, thanks to the prizes handed out during some of the 'bonding' games and exercises we took part in during the day, I went home with $100 more than I went out with.

The business trips didn't end there, and they were always very well funded by Amex. All Special Agents were encouraged to join IAFCI, The International Association of Financial Crime Investigators, and Amex would pay for us to attend its annual conferences. Oh, how awful it was that I was expected to attend the European Chapter's conferences in Ayia Nappa, Corfu, Cyprus, Zurich, Switzerland, Oslo and Norway, and I also attended IAFCI's international conference in Orlando, USA.

Even better was when I got to take Thelma along on a little business trip back in 2005. I had been working on a case involving £250,000 seized from a courier from St. Lucia by UK Customs, which also, like the Gino Hunter case, left me horrified at the incompetence of some of the police officers involved.

Thelma and I already had a trip booked to visit my old friend Doug Taylor in Tobago, so I thought whilst we were there, we could take a side trip to St Lucia to discuss the case with the local police.

Our flight from Tobago was in a twin-engine plane that stopped at three other islands before St Lucia, and we got to observe all the islands as we flew over or landed on them. We arrived in St Lucia and checked into our hotel then headed out to meet the local Detectives I'd made contact with. At their request, I'd booked a steak restaurant, but when we got there, it turned out to be the swankiest, most expensive steak restaurant (again, thanks, Amex!) on the island, and neither of them had been before, so I was already very much in their good books. The meal was fantastic, and the two young men were very forthcoming, though a little hampered on what they could say because of legal restrictions. However, I did gain a bit of useful information, and Thelma and I really enjoyed hearing about life as a St Lucian Detective. After a very enjoyable interlude, we returned to Tobago and our holiday.

It was nice to know my work could sometimes bring good things to Thelma's door.

CHAPTER 7: A LIFE IN SERVICE

I'm not sure how long I expected to stay with Amex, but the 2008 US financial crash took the decision out of my hands. It brought about the closure of the Brighton office, and I chose not to pursue alternative career paths within the company. I took up a position with security firm G4S, but after a short time, it became clear that operations there were very badly organised, so I left.

I was at a bit of a loose end when I spotted an advert in my grandson Cameron's school magazine inviting applications for a lunchtime meal supervisor at £17.50 an hour, but the minimum wage at the time was £7.50. 'It must be a typing error,' I thought, but I was intrigued and phoned the school anyway.

The ad was correct, so I applied and got the job. It was great being at my grandson's school, though I had to be careful not to embarrass him or speak to him too much! After working at the school for a couple of months, the Headmistress sought me out and said, 'You have a bearing about you. How do you fancy being on the Roaming Management Team?' I readily agreed, and from then on, my job was to roam the building, ensure all students were in class, and escort misbehaving pupils to the isolation room. I worked for three hours a day, which was just enough to keep me out of mischief. Happily, I was never called upon to escort Cameron anywhere – in fact, he went on to be Head Boy at the school – and it was lovely to have that little bit of extra insight into his life that, if not for the job, I would not have had.

In 2015, it felt like the time was right for a reunion, so my old digs mate Phil Hall, and I set about contacting old colleagues for what became the West Sussex Constabulary Cadet Reunion. We were able to track down about 120 people who had joined the West Sussex Police Cadets between its formation in 1954 and amalgamation in 1968.

So it was that on 30th October, a great bunch of ex-cadets met up in a hotel in Worthing, and all had a very good time. It was surprising to find that many had gone on to complete their 30 years in policing, which went to show that cadet training had been a pretty good grounding for the job.

We had contacted the BBC to tell them about the reunion, and they sent a cameraman and journalist to roam the room and interview people. I did a bit to camera and told the story of my attempts to get the fingerprints of a dead man in the morgue at Southlands Hospital – but that was deemed to be unsuitable for the teatime news audience, and I didn't make the cut! However, one of our old cadets was a Senior Investigator at the Brighton Bombing, which they found particularly interesting, so footage from our event did make the news in the end.

As the evening wore on, I was surprised to see that Ian Eady hadn't turned up, as he'd been one of the first to accept his invite. I'd been looking forward to seeing him again: having joined as a clerk, later cadet, in 1954, he'd retired as the Chief

Superintendent, and I had never forgotten an incident involving him from back in my early Drug Squad days. Mr Eady (I've always called him that and still do) and I were walking from the court to Chichester Police Station. About 50 yards from the Station, Mr Eady stopped mid-sentence: leaning out of a second-floor window was his Chief Inspector. Mr Eady turned to me and said, 'Look at that bloody idiot! What is he on?!' It was a totally inappropriate way for a Chief Superintendent to talk about a Senior Officer, especially to a Detective Constable, but it was very funny. My eyebrows nearly shot into my hairline, and I've never forgotten it. Ian did turn up later, though by then, nearly all the Old Boys had gone, and we had to tell him what he had missed. The reunion was a success and a great afternoon was had by all. There was much laughter, camaraderie and conversation, as well as 'swinging of the lamp' if you know what that is.

Back in 1967, I swore allegiance to The Queen, and I served her to the best of my ability for 30 years. Of that, I feel proud – and that I may have saved the lives of a few of her subjects along the way.

I never tire of saying I'm a very lucky man. My life has been shaped by unexpected connections, surprises, and enduring friendships. I have formed lifelong bonds with fantastic people and met countless interesting characters, some of whom of a less fantastic persuasion, all of whom have made my journey in law enforcement and beyond a memorable one.

Thelma and I have had a lovely married life and will continue to do so for many more years to come, I hope! We have two lovely children and four beautiful grandchildren we regularly see: Sacha, who is settled with her second husband Phil, who has Cameron and Yasmin; and our son Gary and his wife Lianne have Connor and Josh. We are incredibly proud of them all, and family life continues to be a source of huge pleasure and comfort for me.

Thelma and I have been around the world a few times, having been on countless holidays, including 28 cruises, but now we've decided we're not going on any more. We've seen all the things we want to see. We're contented people, happy to live out our lives in Lancing, and that feels like a great place to be. I wouldn't change one moment in my life, especially those I spent with Thelma, so the last words of this book can only go out to her.

Thank you, my darling Thelma, for everything you have done and everything you endured. I couldn't have done it without you.

DETECTIVE TRAINING COURSE
Initial - 4th February to 3rd April 1980

| J. A. Bacon | P. A. Hellyer | P. J. Roiden | C. B. Brind | B. J. Gibson | C. M. Gillings |
| Det. Cons. | Det. Cons. | Det. Cons. | Det. Cons. | Det. Cons. | Det. Cons. |

| D. J. Bishop | K. G. Scrase | J. W. Lloyd | P. Desborough | D. J. Smith | J. Watkins | G. C. Cannan |
| Det. Cons. | Det. Cons. | Det. Cons. | Det. Cons. | Det. Cons. | Det. Cons. | Det. Cons. |

A. A. Evans   R. C. Bishop   J. Hirst   J. S. Post   G. W. R. Terry, Esq.   C. F. Johnstone   C. L. Leeves   H. D. Reynolds   G. T. Divall

HQ Lewis CID Course.

American Express Global Security, HQ Brighton. Special Agent Yaki Brind, Security Supp Hazel and Ken Betts, Manager.

Lianne Brind, Gary, Yaki, Thelma, Sacha, Phil, Yasmin, Cameron, Josh, Connor and Sadie.

Printed in Great Britain
by Amazon